T0347373

ROUTLEDGE LIBRARY EDITIONS:
THE ECONOMICS AND BUSINESS OF
TECHNOLOGY

Volume 8

COMPANY AND CAMPUS PARTNERSHIP

COMPANY AND CAMPUS PARTNERSHIP

Supporting technology transfer

D. JANE BOWER

LONDON AND NEW YORK

First published in 1992 by Routledge

This edition first published in 2018
by Routledge
2 Park Square, Milton Park, Abingdon, Oxon OX14 4RN

and by Routledge
711 Third Avenue, New York, NY 10017

Routledge is an imprint of the Taylor & Francis Group, an informa business

British Library Cataloguing in Publication Data
A catalogue record for this book is available from the British Library

ISBN: 978-1-138-50336-6 (Set)
ISBN: 978-1-351-06690-7 (Set) (ebk)
ISBN: 978-1-138-57622-3 (Volume 8) (hbk)
ISBN: 978-1-351-27034-2 (Volume 8) (ebk)

Publisher's Note
The publisher has gone to great lengths to ensure the quality of this reprint but
points out that some imperfections in the original copies may be apparent.

Disclaimer
The publisher has made every effort to trace copyright holders and would welcome
correspondence from those they have been unable to trace.

Company and campus partnership

Supporting technology transfer

D. Jane Bower

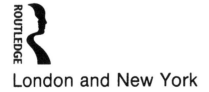

London and New York

First published 1992
by Routledge
11 New Fetter Lane, London EC4P 4EE

Simultaneously published in the USA and Canada
by Routledge
a division of Routledge, Chapman and Hall, Inc.
29 West 35th Street, New York, NY 10001

© 1992 D. Jane Bower

Typeset by Witwell Ltd. Southport
Printed and bound in Great Britain by
Biddles Ltd, Guildford and King's Lynn

British Library Cataloguing-in-Publication Data
A catalogue record for this book is available from the British Library

ISBN 0-415-07080-5

Library of Congress Cataloging in Publication Data
has been applied for

ISBN 0-415-07080-5

Contents

Figures and tables

FIGURES

TABLES

Acknowledgements

The Leverhulme Trust supported research into biotechnology companies' relationships with pharmaceutical companies.

All available published or photocopied information about institutional policies and practices with respect to industrial liaison activities and IPR were obtained from the following, along with specimen copies of standard contract, licensing and other forms, where they are in use:

University of Sheffield Commercial and Industrial Development Bureau.

Mrs June Clark, Director of Industrial Liaison, Oxford University, England.

UMIST Ventures Ltd, University of Manchester Institute of Science and Technology, England.

University of Strathclyde, Scotland.

Harvard University Office for Patents, Copyrights and Licensing.

Niels Reimers, Director of Office of Technology Licensing, Stanford University, USA.

Philip Lemanski, Assistant Director, Office of Science and Technology Development, Columbia University, USA.

H. Walter Haeussler, Vice President, Director Patents and Technology Marketing, Cornell Research Foundation Inc., Cornell University, USA.

William H. Griesar, Vice President and General Counsel, Rockefeller University, USA.

Rodney W. Nichols, Executive Vice President, Rockefeller University, USA.

Material was also obtained from the following, with whom discussions were held, by telephone and/or face-to-face:

Ms Lita L. Nelsen, Associate Director, Technology Licensing Office, Massachusetts Institute of Technology, USA.

Dr Edwin T. Yates, Patent Management Officer, Johns Hopkins University, USA.

Dr David Sturman, the Media Laboratory, MIT, USA.

Professor Anthony L. Redwood, Director, Institute for Public Policy and Business Research, University of Kansas, USA, and Director, KTEC.

Dr Charles J. Decedue, Executive Director, Higuchi Biosciences Center, University of Kansas, USA.

Kevin M. Carr, Vice President, Kansas Technology Enterprise Corporation, USA.

Dr Fred Singleton, Director, Center of Marine Biotechnology, University of Maryland, Baltimore, Maryland, USA.

Dr R. Smailes, Director of Industrial Liaison, University of Dundee, Scotland.

Kenneth Crichton, Director of Industrial Liaison (retired), Heriot-Watt University, Scotland.

I. Grant Ross, Director of Industrial Liaison, Heriot-Watt University, Scotland.

Dr N. H. Reid, Archivist, Heriot-Watt University, Scotland.

Dr Keith D. R. Winton, UnivEd Technologies Ltd, Edinburgh University, Scotland.

Dr R. C. Jennings, Assistant Director in Industrial Co-operation, University of Cambridge, England.

Richard L. Blackmore, Intellectual Property Manager, Industrial and Commercial Development Service, University of Glasgow, Scotland.

Susan Jagers, Industry Liaison, Imperial College of Science and Technology, London, England.

Scott Lawrie, Commercial Section, AFRC.

Paul Gardner, Exploitation Scrutiny Group Secretariat, SERC.

Dr Martin Wood, MRC Industrial Liaison.

Dr Michael Knight and Mr Colin Dale of the BTG and Dr James Green of 3I REL explained the activities of their organisations and supplied documentation.

Ian Dalton, Director, Heriot-Watt Research Park, former Chairman, UK Science Parks Association and former Chairman, Technology Innovation, Information.

Corporate information was obtained from various sources, including the companies themselves. Walter Scott & Partners, Ltd, Edinburgh, kindly made its library of international corporate information and brokers' reports available. Views of the corporate perspective on the relationship were obtained in discussion with:

John Gilmartin, Chairman, President and CEO of Millipore Corp., USA.

John S. Glass, Director, Investor Relations, Millipore Corp., USA.

Brian G. Atwood, Vice President, Director of Operations, Glycomed Inc., USA.

Dr Marshall Myers, Corporate Director, Research and Development, McCormick & Co. Inc., USA.

Mark Berninger, Director, Corporate Development, Life Technologies Inc., USA.

Dr Richard Dennis, Edinburgh Instruments Ltd, Scotland.

David C. Wren, Managing Director, Fermentech Ltd, Scotland.

Peter Swinson, Managing Director, Arcaid Ltd, Scotland.

Dr Roger Gilmour, the Agricultural Genetics Co., England.

Dr Kozo Takahashi, Senior Managing Director, Yamanouchi Pharmaceutical Co. Ltd, Japan.

Dr Isamu Takano, Suntory Ltd, Japan.

Dr Takamoto Suzuki, Manager, Pharmaceuticals Dept Research Planning Group, Kirin Brewery Co. Ltd, Japan.

Dr Akira Imada, Director, Biology Research Labs, Takeda Chemical Industries Ltd, Japan.

Dr Isao Saito, Research Manager, Tsukuba Research Laboratories, Eisai Co. Ltd, Japan.

Thanks are due to all the above for their invaluable help and advice, and especially to Dr Ken Lyall of Walter Scott & Partners for extensive discussion and for reading the manuscript.

Abbreviations

AFRC	Agriculture and Food Research Council
ANVAR	Agence Nationale de la Valorisation de la Recherche
AT&T	American Telephones and Telegraph Incorporated
AUTM	Association of University Technology Managers
BIC	Business Information Centre
BRITE	Basic Research in Industrial Technologies for Europe
BTG	British Technology Group
BVCA	British Venture Capital Association
Caltech	California Institute of Technology
CEST	Centre for Exploitation of Science and Technology
CIS	Center for Integrated Systems
CNRS	Centre National de la Recherche Scientifique
CRITT	Centre Regional d'Innovation de Transfert Technologique
DCS	Distributed Computing Systems Programme
DSIR	Department of Scientific and Industrial Research
DTI	Department of Trade and Industry
EBN	European Business and Innovation Centre Network
EC	European Community
ECLAIR	European Collaborative Linkage of Agriculture and Industry through Research
EEC	European Economic Community
EIRMA	European Industrial Research Managers Association

ERATO	Exploratory Research for Advanced Technologies
ESC Lyon	Ecole Supérieure de Commerce de Lyon
ESPRIT	European Strategic Programme for Research in Information Technology
EUREKA	European Research and Co-ordination Agency
FLAIR	Food-linked Agro-Industrial Research
GEC	General Electric Company, plc
HDTV	High Definition Television
IAB	Innovation Advisory Board
IBM	International Business Machines, Inc.
ICOT	Institute for New-Generation Computer Technology
ICI	Imperial Chemical Industries, plc
IKBS	Intelligent Knowledge-Based Systems
IT	Information Technology
JITA	Japanese Industrial Technology Association
MIT	Massachusetts Institute of Technology
MITI	Ministry for International Trade and Industry
MMI	Man/Machine Interfaces
MoD	Ministry of Defence
MORI	Market and Opinion Research International
MRC	Medical Research Council
NAO	National Audit Office
NASDAQ	National Association of Securities Dealers Automated Quotation National Market System
NEC	Nippon Denki
NEDO	National Economic Development Office
NERC	National Environmental Research Council
NRDC	National Research and Development Corporation
NSF	National Science Foundation
OECD	Organisation for Economic Co-operation and Development
R&D	Research and Development
SBA	Small Business Administration
SERC	Science and Engineering Research Council
SPRINT	Strategic Programme for Innovation and Technology Transfer in Europe
SRC	Science Research Council

TII	European Association for Transfer of Technology, Innovation and Information
UDIL	University Directors of Industrial Liaison
USM	Unlisted Securities Market
VLSI	Very Large-Scale Integration

Introduction

In recent years technology-based companies have experienced a significant increase in the risks associated with product and process development. The rapid rate of technological change, shortening product life cycles, increasing competition and more regulation have all been factors. The time required to develop major new innovations has not shortened; the initial research stage often takes several years, and the design and development stage usually lasts 5-10 years (Freeman 1990). The increasing burden of regulation adds to costs and also to development time, particularly in the pharmaceutical business.

The expenditure involved in bringing a new product to market can be vast. For new drugs, a median estimate is £130m (Freeman 1990; Grabowski and Vernon 1990); for agrochemicals, £40-50m is required (Freeman 1990). AT&T Microelectronics, the US electronic equipment maker, and NEC, the Japanese electronics company, recently announced a joint project to develop a miniaturised memory chip which they expected to cost $440-500m. At the same time there is a growing risk that the actual return from any one product will be markedly less than initially projected, thanks to the intensity of competition.

These pressures are forcing companies to rethink their whole approach to innovation. IBM may still have been able to spend $5.2bn on research and development in 1989, including a 10 per cent slice on blue skies research, but most companies are having to look beyond their own organisation in the search for cost-effective solutions.

The strategic response

Companies have been setting in place strategies to maintain profitability while controlling their exposure to risk. For high technology companies, major investments must be made in long-term R&D projects to develop new products and processes. Maximising returns within an acceptable level of risk is an important objective. Consequently, great efforts are made to reduce the uncertainties of individual projects.

Equally important for firms has been the need to consider the risk characteristics of the stable of projects. The overall risk incurred by the company may be reduced by constructing a carefully balanced portfolio of projects.

The need to manage R&D risk has led to complex strategic planning. These plans often include sourcing of externally generated technology as one of their tactics. This book looks at one of the ways in which companies use externally sourced technology to help maintain a broad range of projects while retaining a degree of flexibility.

The focus here is on the increasing trend towards accessing the expertise and new technology generated in universities and research institutes. It is only one of a number of methods of externalising R&D risk, but it is becoming increasingly attractive to companies. A contributing factor to this growing popularity is the effort now made by most institutions to facilitate university/industry interaction. The questions posed in the book are:

1 What is the experience of technology transfer from universities in the USA and Britain so far?
2 Can we generalise from this to develop models which support more effictive use of existing resources of expertise and inventiveness?
3 How can companies plan to integrate efficiently their internal resources and the alternative possibilities for sourcing new technology in new product development?

Balancing porfolio risk

When planning its portfolio of product development projects, a company must make major strategic decisions about its long-term R&D capabilities. In the first chapter a variety of strategies are described which companies are using to externalise a proportion of innovation-related risk. Their objectives are to reduce the average time horizon of product development, increase flexibility of response to market conditions, and smooth cash flows.

The most significant tactic has been to move from full in-house development of all projects to allocation of a proportion of the portfolio to 'ready-made' or partly developed projects. This is achieved in a variety of ways. One means is to acquire a company along with its proprietary products and projects. Less wholesale methods of accessing external technology include licensing or, most cautiously, acquiring an option to license technology under development.

In Chapter 1 the growth of strategies that include a significant role for sourcing university-generated technology is discussed. An analytic framework for decision-making is introduced. Brief case studies of companies which have employed the strategies described are included.

Acquisition of technology

Chapters 2 to 4 address the first question, with an exploration of the historical origins and the current, complex state-of-play in technology transfer from universities in the UK and the USA. The clash of cultures which has occurred between higher education institutions and corporations is outlined, and the operating frameworks being developed to facilitate interactions between organisations with different cultures are evaluated. There is a fairly detailed examination of the growing markets for technology which have emerged between established companies on the one side and universities, research institutes and small R&D companies on the other. These markets are increasingly international, but there are still considerable national differences.

Indications of success and failure are examined. There are many encouraging stories, but there are also some cautionary tales. The significance of these is considered for managers who wish to decide how potentially rewarding the possibilities are, and how to exploit them effectively.

Chapters 5 and 6 sketch in part of the broader context in which these activities take place. There is a brief description of university/company relationships in other major industrial countries, and a discussion of the role of the university-associated science park. The remaining chapters go on to address the questions of generalisation

from past experience and across frontiers, and the practical conclusions from this for management.

University/company relationships

The cultural incompatibilities of the company and of the higher
education institution which were introduced in the first chapter are
considered in greater detail. Chapter 7 analyses the ethos of the
university on the one hand and the company on the other. An
analysis is made of the possibilities of mutually satisfactory interaction between companies and institutions carrying out basic research
and higher level training. The different organisational cultures and
objectives of universities and companies are compared. How can
these two cultures interact effectively? The implications for their
relationships are considered. Some pointers towards effective
models for decision-making are proposed.

Different environments

Chapter 8 considers some of the difficulties encountered when
attempting to generalise from the American experience of
technology transfer and high technology company development to
the British context. Many of the trends described in this book
originated in the USA, or at least have been best documented there.
Does this body of knowledge and experience offer useful insights to
the rest of the world?

A UK/USA comparison is made of a number of key factors in
the environments for innovation which affect exploitation of
university-derived technology. Some of the factors examined show
significant variation between the two countries. This has importance for decision-making about the routes for developing
university-derived inventions.

The final chapter looks at the track record from the perspectives
of the universities on the one hand and industry on the other. The
conclusion is that there is a great deal to interest companies in
direct relationships with university-based science.

The importance of indirect involvement is also proposed, particularly with reference to the problems of dealing with cultural
compatibility. Small companies with close campus associations
offer a commercial environment which allows large companies to
access indirectly the expertise and novel technology that originates

in the universities. The need to have extensive knowledge of the whole industrial network as it affects innovation is emphasised.

Where to find it?

One complaint met with again and again in talking to managers with responsibility for the company R&D portfolio is 'How do we locate good new product and process ideas and the people who can carry them through to the prototype stage?' Information flows are never perfect, and this is especially a problem in Europe. The Appendix lists some useful information sources for the UK and the rest of Western Europe and offers some pointers on how to locate promising inventions. There are also some suggestions in Chapter 7 on how to plan a fruitful relationship with campus science.

Note on the use of terms

The term 'university' is used to denote all institutions involved in formal provision of higher education and basic research. The terms 'higher education insitution' (HEI) and 'polytechnic' are not used, since they are less widely understood and the latter is about to disappear. 'Research institute' is used to describe organisations whose main activity is basic research. It is understood that such organisations usually have an informal role in provision of highly trained manpower, and may also have a limited role in provision of training at the PhD level.

Chapter 1

Spreading the risk of the company R&D portfolio

New product development is becoming more costly. Markets are becoming daily less predictable. The changes are driven by increasing competitive pressures, technological change and shortening product life cycles.

Technology-based companies, with their long lead times and high R&D costs are looking for strategies which minimise the escalating risks. The same pressures dictate that in order to survive they must stay at the forefront technically. New products are becoming more sophisticated; often they require inputs from several advanced technologies for their development and manufacture. This creates a dilemma. It is imperative to control costs and time horizons; at the same time there is the conflicting need to span an ever-greater technical range.

To reconcile these demands requires a significant modification of traditional strategies. In all industrialised countries and in all sectors, many companies are employing new approaches to address the problems.

HOW COMPANIES INNOVATE

Technology-based industries have traditionally fallen into two major categories in terms of the way they acquire new technology. These have been described as the 'assemblers' and the 'producers' (Barabaschi 1990).

The first are the companies which assemble the product from components made elsewhere. The car and aerospace industries fall into this category. Novel technology generated by subsystems contractors is integrated into the finished product. Rolls Royce, the British aeroengineering company, is typical of the assemblers. Its supplier strategy and R&D strategy are intimately linked. Its skill in co-ordination of in-house and supplier development activity are regarded as one of the key factors for the success of the last decade (FoE 1991).

Chemical and pharmaceutical companies, which manufacture the whole product, fall into the second class. Traditionally they have developed their products entirely in-house, together with the process and manufacturing technologies.

For the first group, the dominant expertise has been in design and integration; for the latter, design and manufacture. The difference has never been absolute. The 'assemblers' may develop some core technology in-house, and indeed this is very important in companies like Rolls Royce. The 'producers' have always used some imported technology in their production processes, and have had to exert a high degree of expertise in integration of functions in product development. However, there has been a substantial, perceived difference of approach for quite a long time.

Now these distinctions are being progressively blurred. New products and processes often involve the integration of several technologies. For companies accustomed to full inhouse development, the burden of maintaining a competitive edge in several technologies is becoming unmanageable. It makes no sense to be reinventing the wheel daily, at great expense, if the required technology, already invented elsewhere, can be bought in at a lower cost. There is not enough time in a highly competitive environment to acquire an in-house capability in a new technology before making use of it. Nor does it make sense to defocus the company's research effort over too broad a range of enabling technologies.

At first sight this seems straightforward, but in reality this is by no means the case. It requires companies to ask themselves the key strategic question 'What business are we in?' more searchingly than ever. It also requires them to answer it with uncompromising honesty about their strengths and weaknesses. This is easy enough when, for instance, a pharmaceutical company is installing a new information system. This requires acquisition of systems and technology developed elsewhere, even if it is customised for the company. The decision to buy in does not cause any profound conflict. The technology required and the function it fulfils have never been perceived as a special area of expertise for the company.

It is much more difficult when the same company must ask itself whether the fundamental technology for making and mass-producing a new product must be bought in, or else accessed through a joint venture with a specialist R&D company. This is the situation which the traditional large drug companies have had to address in the last 15 years. Previously they had regarded the invention, development and much of the production process technology of patented drugs as their core business, and their ability to carry out full, inhouse development was a source of pride and strength. Now they are increasingly acknowledging that while competitive pressures are requiring them to include a significant proportion of extremely novel drugs in their portfolios, it is not cost-effective to try to make all of them in-house. For a variety of reasons, discussed below, it is preferable to source a proportion of their R&D requirements from outside the firm.

R&D risk

There are several sources of risk in product and process development. The company must continually come up with good new product ideas. During the long period of development, cost overruns, time overruns and changes in the external market environment can all add to the uncertainties of revenue projections.

All projects do not necessarily share the same risk profile. Thus one desired objective is to construct a portfolio whose overall risk is minimised by offsetting the risks inherent in the individual projects (Twiss and Goodridge 1989; Bower 1992). The other objective, of course, is to have a stable of projects which will yield an acceptable and steadily increasing level of profit.

How can these aims be reconciled? The company must first identify the nature of the risks it faces, and then consider the alternative ways projects might be organised to control them.

Controlling the risks

What are the risk factors which must be balanced to optimise a company's R&D portfolio? Let us look at them individually, and at the solutions that are commonly adopted.

1 The product doesn't work

This was the problem which led to the abandonment of the British electronics company GEC's military surveillance plane which was to rival the American AWACS.

Technical failure is a risk that is highest at the early stages of development. The maximum risk to the company is when too many projects are at the same early stage. The portfolio should include projects at all stages, from the idea to the finished product – thus there will be a continual flow of new products. If one product fails, the company's position will be relatively protected. Ideally, the company should be involved in as many projects of equivalent promise as can be accommodated within the limits of the budget.

2 Another company brings a better product to market

Speed of product development reduces this risk, as does having as broad a range of products as possible, targeted at different niches.

3 The market may change and demand fails to materialise

This again requires speed and a range of products. Acquisition or licensing of finished products is another possible response.

4 Cost and time overruns

Joint ventures, options to develop alternative products, and a wide enough range of projects to minimise reluctance to axe the less promising, are risk-reducers. Purchase of finished technology removes this risk altogether, at a price.

5 Innovative new enabling technology developed elsewhere threatens the company's competitiveness

This has happened repeatedly in recent years. Many of the most spectacular cases have involved innovative uses of microchip technology. Banks have reduced transaction time and costs. Supermarkets have introduced computerised stock control systems. These changes have permitted quantum leaps in company performance. The possible solutions for competitors are to obtain access to the new technology by licensing etc., or to devise or acquire an even more novel technology.

6 Profitability is threatened because market access is restricted

This has often been the case with Japan, which constitutes a large part of the potential world market for most sophisticated products, but which is notoriously difficult to enter. A common solution is to have joint venture partners who are able to access the part of the market which is closed to the company.

R&D PORTFOLIO STRATEGIES

Companies are responding to these challenges by changes in the way they construct the R&D portfolio. The objective is to reduce average project development time and maximise the total number of projects the company controls, without significantly affecting costs. The company wishes ideally to minimise risks in all categories. The optimum R&D portfolio, then, will contain a number of projects at different stages of development. They will address different market niches, although within the range of the company's other capabilities in marketing, production, etc. They will employ the most effective technologies, whether in-house or acquired by some means. Preferably, there will be a larger number with shared risks and rewards rather than a smaller number with all the risk and all the rewards remaining with the company.

CONSTRUCTING THE OPTIMUM PORTFOLIO

In constructing a portfolio of product development projects, strategic decisions must be made about the number of products that must be on sale at any one time, the range of markets addressed, and the frequency of new product introduction. Internal factors such as the company's in-house capacities, projected growth rates, and required rates of return will influence decisions. The nature of the competition must also be addressed.

The company will have to consider its dependence on external suppliers. This may be for only the most basic raw materials, but there will have to be some assessment of potential problems of ensuring the continuity of these inputs. Where there are abundant alternative sources, there may be no impact on strategic thinking. If, on the other hand, there is a requirement to source relatively complex components, which may require some customisation by suppliers, or a requirement to access technologies developed else-

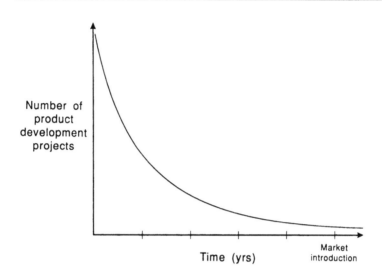

Figure 1.1   Constructing the optimum portfolio

where, then considerations of availability and continuity of supply arise which must be accommodated in the product development strategy. There may be a need to make substantial investment in relationships that are crucial to the success of the strategy (Håkansson 1987).

The optimum portfolio of product development projects will have several characteristics that will ensure a steady flow of products to market. It will contain projects, or options to acquire projects, at all stages of development. There will usually be more at the very early stage than at the near-market stage. Development costs increase exponentially in the course of a normal project, thus it costs relatively little to have a large number at the earliest stage. This allows the company to choose the most promising from among several possibilities before costs start to rise steeply.

All projects need not be in-house – acquiring rights in a project under development in another company can be an acceptable way of retaining an option to part or all of an external project.

At later development stages, development costs escalate. The more promising projects are retained. Again, these may be entirely in-house, or they may involve external partners. Where external partners are carrying part of the risk of the project through investing their own resources, less resources are required from the other partner, reducing its exposure to risk from that particular project. This frees some resources for another project, allowing the company to spread its resources over a larger total number of projects. The potential returns from any one will of course be reduced, but the risks of ultimate failure are also reduced in proportion to the increased number of projects which the company can retain rights in. If one fails to pass the technical review at a later stage of development, more resources can be allocated to the remaining projects. If one fails after market introduction, it is a smaller fraction of the product portfolio and thus less disastrous.

Accessing externally developed technology through licensing or through joint R&D projects is increasingly being treated as just a special case of the client/supplier relationship (Spriano 1989; Håkansson 1987; Pisano 1991; FoE 1991). The supply in these cases is novel technology, technological capability, or even technologically novel products.

Planning to fulfil these technological needs can meet with difficulties on several levels. The first is the reluctance of the company as a whole, and of individual departments, to accept the need for any increase in dependence. It is a blow to the collective corporate ego and can create a sense of vulnerability. Companies may choose to avoid the issue by setting up an in-house capability; sometimes this may be appropriate, but it may on occasion be more costly than other alternatives.

The second level at which problems may arise is that of managing the interface with the supplier. Studies of the efficiency of, for example, Japanese supplier relationships, have underlined the considerable costs incurred in organisations where this interface is mismanaged. Where the relationship to be managed has been created to carry out a joint R&D project, the interface is so complex that organisations often choose to put it into a joint venture company.

The complexity of management problems is at its greatest when several very different organisations are jointly involved in a single product development project. This is the case with projects to develop drugs where several small and large companies in different countries may play complementary roles. Here a group of joint venture agreements are signed, with one of the companies, usually the owner of the intellectual property, acting as one of the two partners in each individual joint venture, but in combination with a different partner for each major geographical market. The other partners contribute finance and often have responsibilities for gaining regulatory approval in their home markets. In return they usually gain marketing rights for the product, restricted to their own market. National regulatory organisations must also input into the process of development, thus creating the need to select partners based in particular countries, which already have relationships with their own regulators.

Where such externalisation of the R&D function is involved, it is essential to consider the full risk implications for the company of entering into relationships with other organisations which may already, themselves, have important relationships with other firms, including competitors. Where development partners have other objectives in addition to those of their own organisation, the tight co-ordination and close communication, which would be optimal for an in-house development, may be entirely inappropriate.

The joint venture agreement permits the project to be separated from the partners by legal boundaries, but the restrictions it creates are not such as to ease the problems of managing the venture. There is inevitably a loss of control of the project, compared with in-house projects, and the provisions of the joint venture agreement must protect both partners. Managers of joint ventures frequently complain that this does not sit easily with the need to set up a structure in which the joint venture can be pursued to a successful conclusion.

Inevitably, for every company the decisions about the component projects in the portfolio and the role of external sourcing of technology requires detailed self-examination about the company's long-term strategy. For every company the answers are very specific to its own situation and aspirations. Decision-making also requires an assessment of the available range of options, including their ability to reduce R&D risk while maximising returns to the company.

The major options which involve significant external sourcing of technology are described below.

The corporate acquisition route

By purchasing a company with its own array of development projects, the acquirer increases its own effective portfolio with a stable of projects at various stages. These can be individually retained, sold or terminated, to tailor the enlarged portfolio of the acquirer to the desired characteristics.

Case study: Plessey, GEC and Siemens

In 1989, Britain's GEC and Germany's Siemens jointly acquired the reluctant Plessey, a medium-sized electronics and telecoms company. They subsequently divided it up. This was a classic example of this strategy. GEC already had a joint venture (GPT) with Plessey, in telecommunications. The takeover was the last step in a leisurely process of technology acquisition.

Large companies may wish to acquire a company, not just for rights to the products and technology, but also for the demonstrated skill of the scientists.

Case study: Lilly and Hybritech

The American pharmaceutical company Eli Lilly's purchase of Hybritech Inc., an early monoclonal antibody diagnostics producer, had this aim. The technology was not proprietary, but commercially oriented scientists with the necessary skills were scarce. By taking over Hybritech, Lilly added this capability to its corporate armoury.

Both of these acquisitions have been widely discussed in the international financial press. In neither case have commentators been able to find any evidence of positive outcomes thus far. The acquired companies in both cases were culturally very different from the acquirers. While this does not necessarily invalidate this method of technology acquisition, it underlines the fact that it can prove very expensive.

Sharing the risk

Alternatives which are much less costly in terms of immediate resources and long-term fixed commitments are also incorporated into the R&D strategy.

In all industries the strategies usually involve externalising some of the risk and reducing the level of in-house product and process developments. In the case of, for example, the pharmaceutical business this has not so far meant abandonment of integrated in-house capability. In-house developments are instead making up a smaller proportion of the new technology associated with new product introductions. In 1988 the main products currently marketed by seventeen of the largest European and American drug companies included only 4 per cent which were not complete, in-house developments (Whittaker and Bower 1991). That figure is a measure of their traditional strategy. Times are changing, though, and their major 'products-in-the-pipeline' in 1988 included 29 per cent of licensed or joint venture projects (Flemings Research 1988).

When it is decided to reduce the overall level of risk by entering into one or more joint projects, what should guide the choice of partners? Preferably, a variety of aims should be served in each agreement. For example, a partner who covers half the costs and does half the development may also be able to access a protected market such as Japan. Splitting the production and marketing rights then involves giving away half of a much larger cake than the original company could have obtained alone.

Capture of innovation-related profits requires that the terms of joint ventures should be drawn up with the relative strengths of the partners in mind. The right partners, the optimum division of responsibilities, and favourable terms for both are important for maximising the overall returns. This is not as impossible as it sounds. Potential partners should complement each other's weaknesses, creating in the joint venture something greater than the sum of its parts.

REAL-WORLD PORTFOLIOS

Do companies manage to achieve these best of all possible worlds in their R&D portfolios? The full details of licensing and joint venture transactions are not revealed publicly. This makes it impossible to assess how closely they approximate to the ideal. Nevertheless, from the information available it is clear that companies are increasingly following the general principles described above. They are balancing their risks and getting added value from their venture partners at the same time.

A typical approach among the large drug companies today is to have several, full in-house projects underway, at different stages on the road to market introduction. In addition to these, there will be a number which have been licensed at very early or intermediate stages, plus some licensed-in as finished products. Similar patterns are found in other industries, although the 'assemblers' already have a firmer tradition of relying on their suppliers for much of the innovation (Håkansson 1987; FoE 1991).

Case study: Novo Nordisk A/S - a niche strategy

In 1989 the Danish companies Novo and Nordisk chose the merger route. They were both medium-sized healthcare companies with strengths in hormonal treatments, particularly diabetic therapy (insulin and delivery systems) and some investment in developing other recombinant DNA blood protein products. The merged company's turnover was in the region of $1.1bn in 1989, with income before tax of approximately $170m. Both had a strong R&D tradition, mainly focused on insulin.

Novo Industri had already in 1988 broadened its technology and product line by purchasing ZymoGenetics Inc., a spin-out from the University of Washington which previously, under contract to Novo, had cloned the insulin genes in a vector designed for production of the human hormone in yeast. An earlier purchase of Novo's was IQBio, a small UK biotechnology company with a useful diagnostic technology. Novo also had a successful industrial enzymes division which was actively acquiring new technology. Nordisk Gentofte was already engaged at the time of the merger in a joint venture with Chiron in San Francisco, to produce Factor VIII for haemophiliacs.

The merged company now holds a very large proportion of the world market for diabetic treatment. It is developing simpler methods of insulin delivery which will also be applicable to the non-diabetic products it has or is developing, expanding its market into other deficiency diseases treated by similar therapeutic regimes.

It continues to maintain a substantial number of other projects in joint ventures with smaller and larger partners. It is co-developing products with Smith Kline Beecham and with Bristol-Myers Squibb, both giants which have likewise chosen the routes of merging with a similar partner and continuing joint projects with smaller companies.

In its 1989 Annual Report, it explicitly states that one of its major advantages is its close relationship with the Danish academic community, and that it plans to establish or expand its research units in the US, Japan, UK and Switzerland, which have close involvement with local university-based science.

Novo/Nordisk is a company which has created a large

diversified portfolio of projects around core inhouse technical and market strengths combined with all the risk-reduction methods described above. It is also extending its expertise in industrial and pharmaceutical protein manufacture into more sophisticated areas of protein engineering. It currently sponsors research at York University, England, on insulin analogues. The company continues research in its own laboratories using the same advanced techniques to modify other therapeutic proteins. In-house research is often closely co-ordinated with external projects. An in-house team working on one of their industrial enzymes, lipase, retains close contacts with researchers at Ireland's Trinity College.

Large companies, with a greater or lesser in-house R&D capability, access externally generated technology in several ways, often at the same time. In Figure 1.2 a large company is acquiring a small, R&D-based company. At the same time it is co-developing a novel product or process with a smaller corporate partner, and maintaining a close relationship between one or more of its project groups and a university-based laboratory. The last relationship may be for a specific product development project, but is more likely to function as a more general technology diffusion arrangement, with the company scientists maintaining close contact with state-of-the-art developments in their field.

The option to license at an early stage

Licensing a finished product minimises risk, but there are drawbacks to this course of action. One is that an appropriate product may not exist, or at least may be unavailable for licensing. The other is that this can be expensive.

It is possible to avoid these problems by searching among the more abundant and cheaper supply of ideas which are at earlier stages of the innovative process. There is still technical uncertainty and development work to be carried out. This has the advantage of allowing product development to be co-ordinated with full, in-house projects. It also allows a larger number of projects to be taken on, with a limited early commitment. At later stages the most promising can be selected. This formula is being applied, with many permutations, by companies across the spectrum of technology-based industry.

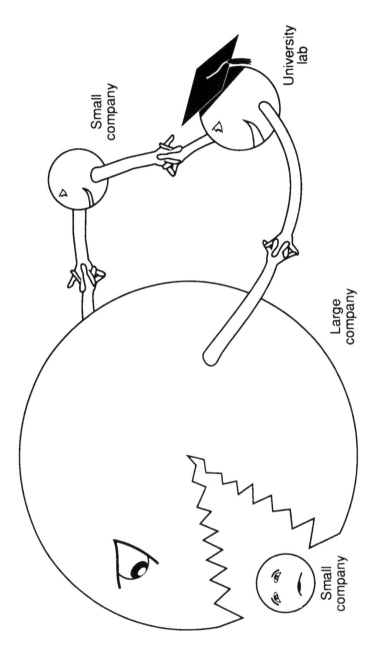

Figure 1.2 Accessing new technology in a high technology industry

The high technology start-up

Sometimes the early-stage product is being developed by a small new company which needs project finance and expertise to carry the product to the market.

With the availability of venture capital to fund technology start-ups, inventors and entrepreneurs frequently choose to set up a new company to develop a novel technology. When they have carried the project to the point at which the potential value is clearly demonstrated, and the in-house expertise is established, they seek corporate sponsorship to support the costly later stages of development.

Windows on technology

Large companies are using these possibilities to acquire 'windows on technology' at early stages of development. They are taking minority stakes in small R&D companies with interesting development projects. In 1990, Silicon Graphics Inc. parted with a 5 per cent stake in return for $35m from the Japanese steel company NKK. The Japanese have been increasingly active in investing in small western R&D companies. Japanese minority investment in US companies grew from forty deals, worth $116m in 1988, to sixty deals in 1989, worth $350m (*Business Week*, 25 June 1990). They are following a continuing trend set by US and European companies, and their capital is very welcome. Lawrence J. Botticelli, the Vice President for business development of Isis Pharmaceutical, a small Californian company, claims that the Japanese are willing to do almost anything in order to be able to participate, including putting in more cash when it is needed (*Business Week*, 25 June 1990).

At the next level of commitment, large companies are becoming involved in joint ventures with small innovative firms, often campus based, to develop specific projects together.

Case study: Genentech & Hoffman La Roche

The Swiss pharmaceutical company Hoffman La Roche purchased 60 per cent of the flagship US biotechnology company, Genentech, in 1989. This followed a lengthy courtship. Roche had already sponsored product developments at Genentech. In this case, both parties agreed to the acquisition, indeed the marriage was solicited by the smaller partner.

At present, Genentech's corporate structure is intact, and will probably remain so even if Roche acquires the rest of the company. Genentech's outstanding in-house expertise in developing and producing novel drugs is likely to assure it a fair degree of autonomy. Roche, for its part, increased the number of its drug development projects by 50 per cent by the purchase.

Know-how trading

A less formal but possibly equally important route for accessing another firm's process innovation is the trading of technical know-how by companies, often rivals. This has been analysed in some detail by von Hippel (1988) in the American steel minimill industry.

Steel minimills use steel scrap rather than iron ore to produce rolled steel. The relatively low capital and materials costs of the process has allowed them to compete successfully with the major integrated steel producers. Some of the American minimills are among the most productive steel mills in the world. While initially they competed in a restricted range of steel products, by continually extending their innovative technology they are penetrating a rapidly increasing number of product markets (Dickson 1991).

Von Hippel studied process innovation in four of the largest minimill companies. Surprisingly, he found that there was a widely recognised pattern of trading know-how between firms. Most of this was very informal, and on a clear basis of reciprocity. It was not unrestricted – company personnel were well aware of areas in which they were willing to trade, and those which they wished to keep secret. Trading occurred with firms that were known to have equal value to offer in return. There was a feeling among company personnel that trading was confined to firms that were not in direct competition, but it was recognised that the information transmitted could then be passed on to others with which there was direct competition. A recent study (Schrader 1991) supports the hypothesis that the transfer was in the interests of all the firms involved.

This sort of distributed, co-operative innovation has been reported by other observers. It appears in the nineteenth-century English industry (Allen 1983) and also in other industries at the present time (von Hippel 1988). The limited reports of its occurrence in the US aerospace and waferboard industries reveal it as a less acknowledged, covert exchange than in minimills, where top management endorsed the practice. In the contemporary semiconductor industry, Rogers (1982) concludes that these informal channels are in fact more valuable than the formal ones for exchange of technical information.

Co-operative trading of know-how among a group of firms that accept the ground rules for the transactions is an inexpensive equivalent of cross-licensing. The speed, informality and inexpensive nature of the arrangement is an efficient way of transferring minor technical information, whose value is not high enough to warrant the costs of formal licensing.

Know-how trading also occurs between firms that have formal joint venture agreements. Along with the precisely formulated exchanges described in the original agreement, there is usually an expectation that the prescribed interactions will be accompanied by other exchanges of information. Some of these will be overt, as part of the mutual desire to advance the joint project where unforeseen problems arise. Others will be incidental to the process of engaging in new activities with a partner who has greater experience of some aspects.

Contract research on campus

There is no certainty that a company will be able to locate externally generated technology to meet its needs. There is yet another alternative to setting up a new, in-house project. In many cases exciting new ideas and technologies are originating on the university campus or in basic research institutes. Companies can access this store of expertise and inventiveness to research and develop new ideas, and direct its general thrust to fit with their own needs. They can also go to the sources of the inventions and sponsor R&D at early and later stages in university laboratories and campus incubator facilities. For a relatively small cost and commitment they can buy the rights to new technology developed in this way, or else an option to license the final product or process. This form of venture also permits the sponsoring company to mould the final characteristics of the product to its own requirements.

When Professor Hartmut Weule became Head of Research and Development at Daimler-Benz in September 1990, one of his priorities was to increase reliance on contract research in universities, with the aim of reducing costs and spanning a wider range of technologies (de Jonquières 1991).

Likewise the Pilkington Group, the British glass manufacturer, whose float glass production technology is seen as one of the major postwar innovations (FoE 1991) states in its Technical Policy Guidelines for Flat Glass Operations: 'With universities, research associations, and suppliers of peripheral technologies, a relationship will be established which reinforces the company's internal technical competence.' Decisions about where to use external resources are based on value analysis and considerations of security.

Company-funded research facilities

A wide range of options are open to companies who wish to access academic skills and invention. Contract research within the university scientist's own laboratory involves the least interaction with the institution.

At the more expensive end of the spectrum are joint research centres set up on or near campuses. They range from what are essentially company labs, with close contacts on campus, to university research labs with some obligations to the company sponsors. The Japanese pharmaceutical company Yamanouchi's English R&D centre near Oxford (announced in 1990) belongs in the first category, as does Kobe Steel's advanced polymers R&D laboratory on the Surrey Research Park. Eastman Kodak's joint sponsorship of the Cornell Biotechnology Center in Ithaca, New York, and the UK Brewing and Distilling Association's sponsorship of the International Centre for Brewing and Distilling at Heriot-Watt in Edinburgh are university research centres, with some specific responsibilities to sponsors.

Formal collaboration in precompetitive research – 'clubs'

Governments in the USA, Europe and Japan are also taking a keen interest in innovation. Aware that technological advantages are of great importance for a country's economic growth, they have all tried to foster the development of new technology.

Joint projects between several industrial partners and often an academic research laboratory are the vehicle favoured by Japanese and European Community (EC) governments for developing technologies through the precompetitive stage. These projects have all the disadvantages that informal information trading avoids. They require extensive planning, supervision and reporting. The partners would probably not have chosen to work together without the financial incentive. The priority areas are set by government.

Japan expects the industrial partners to foot most or all of the bill, but the EC and most of its member countries offer generous support to approved projects, covering 50 per cent of the costs. In Japan and Europe, intellectual property rights are usually shared by the industrial partners. Opinions are mixed as to whether this type of collaboration lies at the heart of Japan's success, or whether industrial success has been achieved there in spite of the government's direction.

The collaborative transnational projects in the EC, and similar projects within member countries, have mostly been set up quite recently. It is not yet possible to assess their impact on companies' competitiveness, but a discussion of the outcomes so far is included in Chapter 6.

THE COSTS OF RISK REDUCTION

Using all these options in constructing a future product portfolio allows companies far more flexibility in response to market conditions. It permits the company to concentrate on the things it does best. It also reduces fixed costs in R&D. It does, however, result in a loss of control over individual projects, and this must be compensated by the added value that partners bring to collaborative ventures. There must be some significant additional benefit to the contracting company to compensate for the additional risk that this loss introduces into the equation.

It also demands new skills of managing collaborative relationships with other organisations. The culture and objectives of the small new company or of the university-based inventor are very different from those of the large company. Large companies deciding to enter into joint ventures with small, R&D-based companies, or to develop new technology on campus, must carefully assess the special needs of these relationships. If these are not addressed, they are unlikely to reap the full rewards.

Some purposes may be better served by indirect relationships. This must be considered on entering into R&D supplier/client relationships with smaller companies and universities. How are the individual participants' relationships with other organisations in the greater industrial network affected? For a large company with a joint venture agreement with a smaller company, there may be indirect access to the academic contacts of the smaller company. The smaller company may have a close and friendly interaction with a university laboratory, through joint projects and shared personnel. This may be an easier way for a large company to deal with academic laboratories assisting a product development than through a direct relationship.

This relates to another problem which may arise when a large company acquires new technology through purchase of a small company. The close relationships the small company had with university scientists or with other small companies may be disturbed. This may lose some of the value which the large company wished to acquire as part of the transaction. Thus acquisition may create unsustainable direct relationships where indirect might have been more sustainable and rewarding.

It is important, then, for companies to have a detailed knowledge of their whole industrial network. This has been emphasised in the studies of collaborative R&D in the Swedish steel, biomedical and other industries (Håkansson 1987; Axelsson 1987; Laage-Hellman 1987). Using a framework drawn from the theory of networking in industrial supplier/client relationships (Hakansson 1982), these studies have analysed the whole industrial network involved in several collaborative innovations. Their work has shown how individual relationships affect other units in the network indirectly. It highlights the value for decision-making of an extensive knowledge of the whole network, developed over substantial periods of time. For companies, this permits a more accurate assessment of the impact any new relationship will have on the whole system, and therefore on themselves. It also supports the crucial decision about what functions should remain entirely in-house, and where externalisation offers genuine net advantage.

The industrial network involved in new product development is depicted diagrammatically from the perspective of a large pharmaceutical company in Figure 1.3. It can readily be redrawn from the perspective of the other units in the network.

A large company developing a new pharmaceutical product is embedded in an industrial network which includes collaborating organisations, competitors, government regulatory agencies, suppliers of finance, and others. The figure shows the network from a

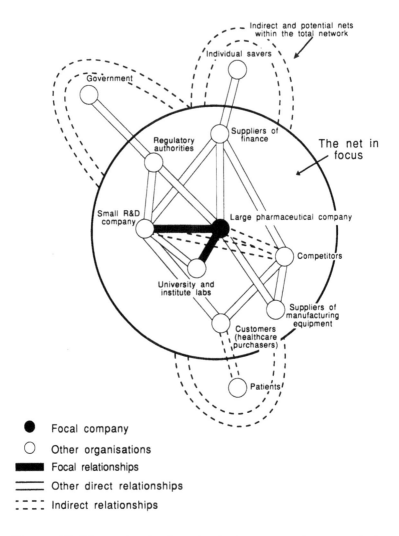

Figure 1.3 The network for developing new pharmaceutical technology

Source: After Axelsson (1987)

large company's perspective. Focal relationships here are with a small R&D company and university laboratories which are all involved in the development. The focal company may have both direct and indirect relationships with some of the other units in the network. Sometimes it will have both with a single unit, if another unit with which it has a direct relationship also has a relationship with the same third party. Indirect relationships with other units are created whenever the focal company forges a new relationship with another unit. These may have implications for competition, indirect access to technology and know-how, etc. It is essential for the focal company to have extensive knowledge of the network as a whole, if it is to manage its own relationships to best effect.

TECHNOLOGY TRANSFER – THE HISTORY AND PRESENT SITUATION

Where does university-generated technology and expertise fit into this picture? In the next few chapters, the history of technology transfer from universities to companies in both the USA and the UK is traced from the turn of the century to the present. The conflicts of interest and other problems faced by specific higher education institutions and research institutes are recounted, along with the solutions that institutions are evolving to facilitate these relationships.

Chapter 2

The new approach to company/ campus joint ventures

The traditional view that universities' activities should be confined
to the teaching and basic research functions has been evolving
towards a much broader view of the role and responsibilities of
academia.

Developments in the USA have influenced British perceptions of
the importance of campus-derived technology. In recent years there
has been some convergence of opinion in the two countries as to
what constitutes an acceptable pattern of interaction between
industry and academia. This has given rise to extensive discussion
about the relationship between universities' organisation and
culture and their ability to meet any particular set of policy
objectives. Although the broader environments for innovation in
the USA and the UK are widely divergent, at the level of the
universities most of the recent stages in the evolution of mechanisms for technology transfer show many similarities.

THE SOURCES OF INVENTION

The period 1945–75 saw a vast expansion in public support of
scientific research in both the USA and the UK. Postwar governments believed that science and technology held the key to future
economic prosperity. The accepted role of the public sector was to
provide much of the skills and the broad knowledge-directed
research base. This was the foundation on which industries were
expected to build new process technologies and commercial products. There was little questioning of the clear distinction believed
to exist between this 'basic research', sponsored by society as a
whole, and applied research oriented towards process and product
development. Industry was expected to play its part by underwrit-

ing the applied research which would bring new technologies to the marketplace.

University scientists regarded themselves as an elite, charged with the mission of carrying out creative, basic research for the general good of mankind. Applied research was less prestigious and was regarded as demanding less outstanding talents. It was perceived as offering a less worthy challenge to the ambitious young scientist. The lower salaries on offer for research posts in the public sector were balanced by their greater prestige and security.

This view of the scientific order was shattered by a series of events. In 1973 scientists at Stanford and San Francisco State published their technique for the construction of recombinant DNA (Cohen *et al.* 1973). This was followed by the filing of a patent application to protect its exploitation. The subsequent formation in 1976 by one of the scientists, Herb Boyer, and a venture capitalist, Bob Swanson, of Genentech (the flagship company of 'the Biotechnology Revolution') initiated the transformation of academic attitudes towards commercially directed research (see Chapter 3).

Genentech was set up to develop and market a new generation of drugs identical with natural effector molecules in the human body. The expectation was that these would be free of the troublesome side-effects which diminished the usefulness of conventional drugs. These novel products were made possible by the powerful new techniques of molecular genetics, of which Cohen *et al.*'s (1973) was one of the first to be reported.

These were key events in the chain which changed the perception of the role of basic research and its relationship with companies' R&D. Much of the distinction between 'basic' and 'applied' was blurred. The new companies which sprang up in the wake of Genentech to develop novel drugs and other products had their roots in universities. They maintained these connections very publicly in order to keep the inflow of equity funding generated by popular faith in their technical virtuosity. Some of the new companies equalled the top university laboratories in scientific prestige.

Genentech and many of the other biotechnology companies in the USA continually incorporated state-of-the-art technology directly from university laboratories into their in-house labs. Instead of retreating into corporate secrecy, their scientists remained part of the small interactive groups of leading researchers in their discipline. They continued to contribute papers on their own innovative work to the group. In return, they drew constantly on the intellectual resources of the wider scientific community, integrating the newest techniques into their development work.

The big international drug companies were left behind. They had few proprietary projects as promising as the novel therapeutics under development in the new companies. In order to acquire a share in the small companies' innovative products, some of them underwrote their vast development costs (about $100–230m per new drug) in exchange for limited licensing rights in the finished products. The new companies managed to maintain their independence by skilful financing strategies. They avoided too close ties with a single sponsor, each preferring to involve several large companies in agreements to fund development costs, in exchange for licensing rights in different markets.

The impact on attitudes

Several important changes in attitudes towards basic scientific research took place, initially and most strongly in the USA:

1 University basic research laboratories were seen to be the direct source of some of the most exciting, industrially relevant technologies. This perception was shared by scientists, companies and venture capitalists.
2 It was now accepted that the chasm dividing the cultures of university and industrial laboratories could be bridged where both sides were sufficiently motivated, enabling the transfer of technology.
3 Belief in the importance of innovation for economic progress, coupled with a stagnant economic outlook, led government bodies, large companies and other interested groups to address the problems of accessing academic inventiveness.
4 The elections of Ronald Reagan in the USA and Margaret Thatcher in the UK initiated a period in which increased pressures from government, along with other environmental factors, accelerated the rate of change in the cultural values of science. Privatisation wherever possible became the rule, industrial liaison became a respectable activity for academic scientists, and profit-making became highly acceptable to everyone.

European reactions

While new companies in the USA were raising hundreds of millions of dollars in equity and joint venture finance, European scientists and policy-makers were also responding, although rather slowly. The science base was there, but the business environment was hostile to start-up companies.

Sources of finance for new ventures were very restricted in Europe. The American companies were able to tap the substantial US venture capital markets for seed finance. They could go on to raise public equity capital at an early stage through the large, well-developed OTC markets. No equivalent existed in Europe at that time. Stock exchanges in general were small and parochial. The only exception, the London Stock Exchange, specifically excluded very new companies. It required a 5-year trading record and a very large cash outlay to satisfy its regulations from any company seeking a listing. Where the USA had well-developed capital markets for all stages of company development, Europe had gaps which made it very difficult for a small company to raise the funds necessary for ambitious, long-term R&D projects.

The British failure to innovate

In the UK, in particular, there was chagrin at the speed with which Americans were moving to exploit new technologies. Some of the main technical advances in biotechnology had been made in British laboratories, notably Kohler and Milstein's (1975) technique of constructing monoclonal antibodies. This was never patented because the official body charged with exploitation of public sector inventions could see no commercial application. Its potential was speedily spotted and it is now the basis of a billion dollar diagnostics business, mostly benefiting non-UK companies. The story was the same in the case of the more recent invention of amorphous silicon at Dundee University, which created the possibility of making cheap photovoltaic cells to convert solar power. This is being successfully exploited in Japan and the USA (MacKenzie and Jones 1985; Bain 1991). British failure to exploit its own abundant inventiveness was castigated again.

The logistics of getting inventions out of the universities and into companies was becoming a major focus of interest in the UK, as in the USA.

Changing pressures

In both the USA and the UK, the pressure for closer university/industry relations came from several directions. Public funding for university research was plateauing in both countries. This was driving universities to seek alternative sources of finance.

Governments in the stagnating economic conditions that followed the postwar boom were looking for new engines for economic growth. Industrial innovation was the prime candidate, and universities were proving to be a significant source. Companies under pressure to bring more technologically sophisticated products to market were looking for new solutions. Inhouse R&D increasingly had to be supplemented by acquired technology. Strong forces were impelling closer collaboration between industry and universities.

The technology transfer debate

Not everyone saw the natural logic of industry tapping the universities' skills. The closer interactions between business and academe which began in the second half of the 1970s were greeted with a mixed response. In many quarters it was felt that the independence and integrity of academics were threatened (Meyerhoff 1982; Moses 1985), with the most vocal protests coming from the USA. Critics included university scientists, administrators and industry personnel (Pajaro 1982).

Strong reservations were voiced about the long-term impact on the universities' training function. There were fears that research areas with less direct commercial appeal would suffer. It was predicted that permitting some academics to spend a substantial proportion of their time on profit-oriented activities would create problems of morale among their colleagues.

The debate about the changing role of the university in society has not been completely resolved. There is a broad international consensus that the skills and inventive power of academic scientists must serve the greater good of mankind, but opinions vary as to the best way of approximating this ideal. It is now generally accepted that a close institutional involvement in technology transfer is legitimate, and can be reconciled with other activities (Moses 1985; Sproull 1985). The conflicts predicted have materialised to some degree, but they are now addressed pragmatically rather than ideologically. University/industry collaboration is now an important theme in the USA, Europe and Japan.

The decision that closer collaboration with profit-making organisations is appropriate has been succeeded in most places by a highly empirical process of developing effective institutional frameworks and procedures. This is still in progress, and the general formulas which are beginning to emerge are likely to remain flexible in many respects to cope with the varied nature of the problems. The procedures are quite diverse, in line with the diversity in size, orientation and type (e.g. state or private) of institutions. There are substantial national differences thanks to the different roles of the various types of higher education institutions and their historical relationships with industry.

Incentivising innovation

While innovation had not originally been a major focus of university policy, there was already some provision in the UK and the USA for dealing with university inventions. Modern molecular genetics-based technologies were not the first important inventions made in university laboratories. The patenting of the process of irradiation enhancement of vitamin D in natural products by the University of Wisconsin generated sufficient royalty income to make Wisconsin a major international biochemical research centre. Research Corporation, a non-profit organisation assisting university technology exploitation, was set up in 1912 with funds generated by the patents concerning electrostatic precipitators invented by Cottrell, a chemist at University of California at Berkeley. This was the first organisation to act as a technology broker between universities and industry.

In the UK, discoveries such as the cephalosporins, first investigated at Oxford's Dunn School of Pathology, and Southampton University's cyclone technology for separating oil and water, are just two of many earlier university-based inventions which were correctly evaluated and exploited.

Already in 1968 the National Science Foundation of the USA had published TRACES, Technology in Retrospect and Critical Events in Science (NSF 1968), its detailed study of the events which had led to six major innovations in different industries. It found that 70 per cent of the key events took place in the course of basic research. Only 20 per cent occurred during mission-oriented research and the remaining 10 per cent during development and application. While most of the events took place some time before the innovations were introduced to the market, some happened right up until the last months before product introduction.

A later study (Gellman Associates 1976) looked at a large number of innovations derived from university research during the period 1953–73. The average lag from invention to product or process commercial introduction had shortened to 7.2 years.

Governments in Britain and the USA, recognising that significant, patentable inventions were sometimes made in the course of publicly funded research, had laid down official routes for exploitation. However, both the recognition of commercial potential of research findings and subsequent development were agreed to be inefficient. US universities argued that their own record of exploitation, where they were given control of IPR, was much better than that of the official routes. In the UK, cases such as the failure to patent monoclonal antibody technology demonstrated that important inventions were being missed.

In the USA until 1980 and in the UK until 1985, government held first option to all rights in IPR generated in the course of the research it sponsored. Where these rights were exercised, there was rarely any possibility of reward for the inventor or for the inventing institution. This gave them little incentive to identify commercial potential. This had two unfortunate effects from the point of view of exploitation. The first was that it reduced the probability that any industrial potential would be recognised. The second was that valuable inventions were not patented. In some cases this led to potentially valuable inventions never being exploited, since the costs involved required proprietary protection to ensure an adequate return to the company underwriting development. In other cases, inventions were exploited to the great profit of companies which had borne none of the cost of the invention, as in the case of monoclonals.

Expecting that with the prospect of some reward, they will be more successful in identifying uses and potential licensees for their technology, the inventing institutions have been given rights in their IPR, with minimal restrictions. For the same reason, institutions now usually give a reasonable proportion of net royalties to the inventors.

In the USA, universities have continued to try to increase their rights in their own IPR, including inventions generated with industrial sponsorship. There is evidence of a similar trend in the UK, although it is accompanied to a greater extent by the use of other exploitation routes, including technology brokers.

Active transfer

Transfer of technology from the laboratory to industry is widely reckoned to be more efficient where the inventors and/or institutions play an active role. Acknowledging this, most universities and other research-based institutions have increased their direct involvement in technology transfer, at least in the early development stages. Policies and organisational structures have been emerging to facilitate this activity and to integrate it acceptably with other institutional functions.

In the following chapters a detailed examination is made of technology transfer policies and structures at a substantial sample of UK and US institutions, including some of the most highly regarded research universities. It reveals close parallels in the problems encountered and in the empirical solutions that are developing.

In both countries a small number of institutions with a long history of successful industrial collaboration have been a source of models for most of the rest. However, differences in the level of institutional commitment to research and other factors have led to some variation in individual approaches. The trend is towards developing relationships with industry with several levels of mutual commitment, through consultancy, sponsored research, and joint ventures. Structures with varying degrees of formality coexist. They range from industrial affiliate programmes – fairly informal associations between several companies and a school or faculty to permit contacts and information flow – to formal collaborations with a contractual basis, for specific product development projects.

The spectrum of interactions with corporate culture is creating a more mature commercial consciousness among researchers. It is enhancing their ability to gauge the value of their skills to companies and to assess the industrial potential of their technology.

Most universities have set up offices and engaged professionals to interface with industry. The American Association of Technology Managers (AUTM) grew tenfold between 1975 and 1987. The British University Directors of Industrial Liaison (UDIL) group now includes representatives from nearly all the UK universities.

This is a measure of the growth of planned co-operation with industry. These organisations meet regularly to share ideas and experience. The US meeting also attracts a large number of interested company representatives, eager to hear of new technology which might be useful to them.

Campus start-ups

There is also an international movement towards university involvement in start-up companies, and in joint venture companies set up with an industrial partner. These are considered by an increasing proportion of institutions as appropriate vehicles for developing university inventions. Consortia of companies, in the USA often with state support as well, have joined universities in setting up major campus development centres, particularly in microelectronic and biotechnology-associated technologies. These will be considered in some detail in later chapters.

In both the USA and the UK many universities now offer seed capital, incubator and science park facilities. Again, these facilities are usually financed by a consortium, including the institution, the state or local government and an independent private partner. This last might be a venture capital firm or one or more large companies, looking for a window on new technology.

Often the institution or the consortium may be willing to take equity stakes in these ventures. Where there is university-owned IPR, equity may be taken in place of royalties.

Transatlantic comparisons

Apart from a slight delay in the onset of widespread academic interest in the UK, the main differences between the USA and the UK in this area appear to be due to external factors. UK universities are more unanimous in their official commitment to exploitation than are some of their American counterparts. Some of the private US universities such as Harvard and Rockefeller are still very concerned to preserve academic freedom by keeping outside influences at arm's length. However, in general there is not a great difference.

The similarity is much less where the attitudes of industry are concerned. Industry in the UK has much less interest in university/industry collaboration than has the American corporate sector. Oxford University is one of the more successful in attracting industrial funding, but four-fifths of this comes from foreign companies (Clarke 1989a). Its 1988 start-up, Oxford Glycosystems, is mainly backed by the American company Monsanto (Clark 1989b).

Case study: Monsanto and Oxford Glycosystems Ltd

Monsanto, the American chemical and pharmaceutical major, is one of the most active companies in taking options to biotechnology-derived innovation in all its shapes and forms. It backs companies developing environmentally friendly pesticides, companies putting genes into plants, and companies developing novel drugs.

One of its more interesting recent corporate ventures is the company Oxford Glycosystems Ltd, which Oxford University and Monsanto set up in 1989 to exploit Raymond Dwek's work on carbohydrates. Five researchers from G.D. Searle, a Monsanto subsidiary, work with Dwek. Monsanto has funded the research since 1983 and has great hopes of the therapeutic potential of carbohydrate compounds. It also supports carbohydrate research in Washington University, Saint Louis.

Glycobiology is a very new area of research with rather few centres of expertise. If its promise materialises, in addition to any products of these ventures which make money, Monsanto will have built itself a very powerful skills and knowledge base for further exploitation.

The general UK business environment is more hostile than the US for start-ups, for many reasons, some of which are discussed in Chapter 7. Another factor of importance not discussed below is the lack of management with relevant business skills. It is generally agreed that this has resulted in UK technology start-ups being underfunded and less well-managed relative to their American counterparts (Arthur Young 1988). Very few have had ambitious, long-term development plans on the lines of Hewlett-Packard, one of the earliest Stanford spin-outs, or Genentech and Amgen, two of the 1970s biotechnology start-ups in the USA. Those which have, have not yet achieved their objectives.

Incentivising the inventors

As remarked above, innovative success does not offer rewards within the conventional university career structure. On the whole it tends to conflict with the requirement to publish and otherwise disseminate information about research as quickly and freely as possible.

Where worldwide patent protection is sought, publication must be delayed. In the hypercompetitive world of science, this carries career costs. Similarly, the time required to carry an invention forward to the point at which it can be integrated into a company's technology may be spent at the expense of traditional academic pursuits. These, together with publication records, are the activities most likely to result in university promotion and scientific recognition.

This has been recognised both in the UK and the USA as a significant barrier to effective technology transfer. Where scientists have no interest in exploitation of their work, its potential is unlikely to be meaningfully assessed and realised. Where they do become involved in further research with a sponsor who wishes to exploit their invention, the outcome is less likely to be favourable if their time and attention is divided between the technology transfer project and other projects which more effectively advance their careers. There are no perfect solutions to this problem, but some progress has been made towards finding compromises which are satisfactory to all parties.

Inventors can now expect financial rewards in fair proportion to the royalty income from inventions. Some institutions invest a share of the residual royalties in inventors' laboratories, which does offer indirect career assistance. For some inventors, the answer is a career change, moving to a company, sometimes with a substantial equity stake, to commercialise the invention. An increasing number of universities are allowing staff some freedom to come and go between industry and their institution, while they decide which direction they wish to follow.

There has also been some change in attitudes, allowing a fair measure of prestige to attach to success in the various activities of industrial liaison, but how this is affecting career prospects is still fairly nebulous.

THE RESPONSE TO THE NEW CHALLENGE

Policy development

On the whole, the institutions that have had longstanding ties with industry have travelled farther down the path towards developing a wide range of formal and informal services and facilities for their clients. They usually have better-evolved systems for disseminating information to all interested parties. Their marketing strategy is directed both inwards at their own members and outwards at potential sponsors. Less-experienced institutions do not always appreciate the need for this.

Cornell, MIT and Stanford in the USA fall into the first category. UMIST, Imperial College and Edinburgh University are among the British institutions which also qualify for this description. The others are tending to scan the practices of the pioneer institutions for successful models. Where these fit with the university's own perceived needs and capabilities, they are usually adopted. In the UK, some direction from central government has also had an influence.

The precedents

Cornell, originally a land grant college and now partly state university, partly elite private school, sees it as an integral part of its mission to serve the technical and social needs of society (see Chapter 5). It plays an active role in technology transfer, encouraging the setting-up on campus of special company-sponsored organisations for this purpose, such as the Biotechnology Center. It has a science park and encourages close interaction between venture capital firms, large and small industrial companies and academics.

Rockefeller, a private institution, places fundamental research for the good of mankind firmly at the centre of its mission, with industrial liaison as secondary to this. It strongly supports the importance of technology transfer, but is anxious to protect the independence of its scientists. 'Science push' drives their activities, rather than commercial pull.

British universities are also influenced by their established image, although not exclusively. Oxford has an extremely positive and practical approach to exploitation of its technology, including a strong commitment to assist in new company formation. Cambridge University, which has been most successful over a long period in generating start-up companies, has one of the most *laissez-faire* approaches. It justifies this, not unreasonably, on the grounds that it has worked very well so far. The point about which it is most emphatic is its desire to encourage inventors to take a very active role in exploiting their invention. It is prepared to be very relaxed about time spent in this way, believing it to be of prime importance for effective technology transfer.

The importance of the 'champion'

This involvement of the inventor in further development is pinpointed by other, experienced university Technology Transfer Directors as crucial to success. Where a large company is also involved in the transfer, an influential 'champion' on the company side is also regarded as very important (Nelsen 1988a). This pivotal relationship at the interface between company and campus is one of the less formalisable aspects of the innovation process. Most institutional policies permit it, but few emphasise it sufficiently.

The more experienced university Directors of Technology Transfer are very aware of the daunting difficulties of taking the invention through this interface to the point where it can be integrated completely with the company's existing technologies and systems. Without considerable commitment by the inventor and the company executive in charge of the project, the innovation process is unlikely to be carried to a successful conclusion. The reality is usually very remote from the popular scenario of industrial spies stealing an invention and fleeing with it, ultimately making a fortune at the expense of the unfortunate inventor.

TECHNOLOGY BROKERS

Patenting and licensing require an array of specialist expertise which it is expensive for an institution to retain inhouse. Policing exploitation agreements and pursuing infringers of intellectual property rights also require considerable resources. For smaller, less well-endowed institutions in particular, the costs of inhouse provision may be unjustifiable.

Licensee's liability for these expenses is sometimes written into licensing contracts: this is more common in the USA. The alternative is to use the services of a technology broker. This is an organisation which takes possession of the IPR, protects and licenses it. In exchange, it pays a proportion of royalties to the inventing institution. This is usually 50 per cent of royalties, net of the broker's costs.

Technology brokers normally have extensive inhouse skills in evaluating, patenting and licensing new technologies. They usually have longstanding relationships with potential licensee companies around the world. For a company looking for exploitable ideas, they are certainly worth contacting. They are easy to access and it is a relatively inexpensive way to scan a large number of potential projects. Even if they are unable to offer any interesting licensing opportunities, they are a source of useful information about where and how good technology may be located. They also have a great deal of experience in working at the interface between academia and corporation, and they have a great deal of insight into the practical problems which arise.

USA

In the USA, several private organisations are in operation, of which the best known is probably Research Corporation. It was set up by Professor Fred Cottrell to patent and license US university inventions. When Sir Solly Zuckerman visited the USA in 1946, he was extremely impressed by its success. When he returned to Britain, he recommended that the British government set up a similar organisation. It was in response to this that the NRDC was set up. This was a government body which had first option to exploit government-sponsored inventions. This monopoly was retained by its successors until 1985, when it was taken away from the British Technology Group (BTG), in order to encourage universities to play a more active role in exploitation.

The BTG

Since the removal of its first refusal rights, the BTG has remained a very important player in British university technology licensing. It has accumulated a considerable body of specialist expertise in assessing the commercial potential of inventions, finding licensees and policing patents. It recently successfully pursued the US Department of Defense in the American courts for employing BTG-held technology in hovercraft without a license. The $6.1m award gave favourable publicity to the BTG.

Range of operation

At any one time, the BTG offers 1,500–2,000 licensing opportunities. These are mainly in areas where it expects the invention to have a large and accessible market. One of its preferred areas is healthcare, which is dominated by a small number of large companies, simplifying the search for a licensee. Where previously it was required to try to license any invention presented to it by an institution, now it will only consider inventions which it expects to have a major international market.

Thus, companies looking for very specialised technology which might not meet this criterion should talk directly to researchers. However, BTG's interests range from hydrocyclone separation of oil/water mixtures, through pharmaceuticals to High Definition Television (HDTV) technology, so it is important to include it in any technology search.

The role of the broker need not prevent a company from seeking a direct relationship with the scientists working with the technology. When licensing a BTG-held invention, a company may still choose to seek assistance in development from the inventor.

The BTG is scheduled for privatisation and is expanding its activities. It now provides a certain amount of seed capital and plays an active role in some of the on-campus development organisations in the UK. It is also a collaborative partner in a number of projects on crop protection along with government research institutes and the Royal Botanic Gardens at Kew.

It is extending its search for commercialisable ideas farther afield. In the USA it recently opened a new office in Gulph Mills, Pennsylvania. It has also been invited to handle intellectual property issues arising from projects supported by the European Institute of Technology in universities throughout Europe. The EIT was recently formed by an industrial consortium of major companies to fund selected research projects within European academic institutions and to stimulate industry–university co-operation. It is also a participant in EUROTECH (see below).

3I REL

Another technology broker active in the UK is 3I Research Exploitation Ltd. It is owned by the major venture capital company 3I plc. It started out as a joint venture between Research Corporation and 3I, but Research Corporation withdrew from the arrangement last year. It has very close relationships with several English universities.

The EC

All the countries of the EC have government organisations which have responsibility for technology transfer. There is now an EC programme, EUROTECH, whose objective is to create a network among them. Thus companies will be able to access all members' available technology through, say, the BTG.

Addresses of the above and information about other organisations within Europe which are active in technology brokering are in the Appendix.

CENTRAL DIRECTION OF TECHNOLOGY TRANSFER POLICY

In the UK there have also been some efforts by government to smooth the passage of university-derived innovation. Traditional and institutional barriers inhibiting innovation have been identified within government and between the public and private sector (Wallard 1984).

Committees have been set up to look at the question of how best to facilitate commercialisation of university and research council inventions. They have issued several reports offering guidance to institutions on general aspects and also on local issues: the position of Britain in the European Community poses some special problems, especially where EC-funded research is concerned (DTI 1989). Apart from this, the policy trends at institutional level in the USA and the UK are similar, in spite of the very different business environments.

In both countries, government has also taken a steadily more proactive approach to organising major collaborations between industry and academia in the area of precompetitive research. These programmes have been directed towards improving national competitiveness in what have been identified as strategically important generic technologies.

EFFECTIVE PRACTICE

It is too early for a proper evaluation of the efficacy of the procedures that have been adopted. However, the initial results are very encouraging. In both countries, industrial sponsorship and income to universities from licensing IPR is on a rapidly rising trend. This reflects in part the more active approach institutions are taking towards attracting alternative sources of research funding, in part the more aggressive attitude towards control of their IPR. Nevertheless, it probably also indicates that there is now more efficient transfer of technology in academic environments whose awareness of industry's needs has been sharpened.

In 1989, the total income from US university and government laboratory licensing of IPR was around $45m compared with £25m or $47m royalty income to the British Technology Group. These figures and their implications are discussed further in Chapter 8. It suffices to note here that they do not imply that university invention has been less well exploited in the UK than in the US. If anything, they suggest the reverse.

It has been observed that universities' licensing income is very small compared with contract research funding. The implication is that it is not really very important. This disregards the fact that it ends up in different budgets, where it may in fact be very significant. The inventor's share is likely to be a noticeable, occasionally spectacular addition to a scientist's earnings. The university's share is applied as the university or department sees fit, unlike most institutional income. The incentive value of royalties must be considered in this context.

The number of company/campus joint ventures is steadily rising, involving both start-ups and established companies. Some of these will be considered in more detail in the following chapters, which look at the evolution of technology transfer from American and British universities from the beginning of the century up to the present.

The current generation of joint ventures, often very ambitious undertakings with substantial industrial support, is frequently the most recent stage of a longer-standing relationship. The willingness of the parties to enter into further, more public commitments argues a degree of satisfaction with the initial phase of the relationship. This can be taken as indicative of the success of the earlier ventures. They are signs that the new approaches are working for both the universities and for industry.

Chapter 3

Technology transfer on the US campus

THE ESTABLISHMENT OF AMERICAN ASCENDANCY IN SCIENCE AND TECHNOLOGY

Until the First World War, the USA was a follower in the world of science. In the early days its institutions were set up in the mould of the most prestigious European models of the time. With the coming of the war, academic and industrial scientists and engineers were brought together to solve urgent military problems. The war was also a period of isolation from European influences. These experiences speeded the emergence of an effective and characteristic structure for research. American science began to develop a distinctive style which was eventually to combine its growing science and technology strengths.

After the war, much of the close co-operation was lost, but major changes had already taken place. Not the least of these was the growing public perception of the utility of science. This contributed to the universities' ability to attract funds for research and training from many sources. By the end of the 1920s, the USA was on an equal footing with any other nation in general scientific eminence. Then came the influx of European intellectuals and scientists, escaping from fascist regimes. This decisively weighted the balance in America's favour. By the time the Second World War broke out, the USA was unquestionably the centre of world science.

The history of this evolution offers fascinating insights into the process which forged America's might in twentieth-century science and technology.

THE FOUNDING OF THE AMERICAN RESEARCH UNIVERSITIES

During the latter part of the nineteenh century, there was a great deal of debate about the nature of the activities desirable and appropriate for major American universities.

Science began to make inroads into the classical curriculum of American universities in the mid-nineteenth century, but the first formal attempt to establish utilitarian teaching in higher education was the Morrill Act of 1862. This granted a substantial tract of federal land to each state to maintain colleges where the main subjects taught would be 'agriculture and the mechanic arts' (Hofstadter and Smith 1961). The availability of these funds led directly to the founding of the state universities of Illinois and California. In New York State, Ezra Cornell's gift of $500,000 was put together with the state's land grant, creating Cornell University in 1868.

The foundation of Johns Hopkins University in 1876 was another milestone in the evolution of the American research university. The advances of Germany's science and the role of its academic institutions were demanding the attention of the world. Johns Hopkins' objective was to offer advanced education of an equivalent standard to that available in Germany at the time. In pursuit of this aim, Johns Hopkins encouraged its faculty to engage in research as a routine part of their work. The scale and success with which this was undertaken influenced the higher education debate of the time. By 1890, Johns Hopkins' goals were shared by several other institutions.

1900–20

Through the first two decades of the twentieth century, fifteen universities established themselves as major research centres. Several of these were state universities:

Harvard
Columbia
Chicago
Cornell
Johns Hopkins
California
Yale

Michigan
MIT
Wisconsin
Pennsylvania
Stanford
Princeton
Minnesota
Illinois

This was a period of great economic growth, paralleled by the growth in demand for higher education. The state allocations to the main state universities increased fourfold in real terms between 1900 and 1920 (Geiger 1986), while their tuition income was a less significant source of funds, at about 25 per cent the rate per head charged at most of the private universities.

The research universities also increased their incomes. Their wealth came fairly equally from private endowments and from tuition income (except for Johns Hopkins and Stanford, which did not rely heavily on tuition fees until after 1920).

Two individuals overshadowed all other philanthropists in their abundant donations to higher education: John D. Rockefeller and Andrew Carnegie. They both founded major universities and research institutions, and gave freely to existing universities. In total, they each donated hundreds of millions of dollars to higher education (Lester 1941; Fosdick 1952).

The universities, many of which had already received major benefits from these and other wealthy philanthropists of the time, began a continuing programme of organised fund-raising from foundations, and from their growing numbers of successful graduates. These sources provided a steady growth in general university funds at the institutions most committed to research.

University research support 1900–20

Over this period there was a trend towards earmarking faculty-controlled funds for research purposes. This was by no means universal, however. A 1921 survey only managed to find nine universities that operated such a system.

An equally significant form of research support was the increasing time available to university staff to engage in research. Staff/student ratios improved, teaching hours fell and sabbatical leave became common. These improvements were all instituted to give staff the opportunity to do more intensive research.

As the great research universities grew and their departments established strong reputations, their links with the surrounding community diminished. The social worlds of the academics and the local community became less interconnected. The needs of the university became less of a focus for local philanthropy. This ceased to be a significant source of support in the second decade of the twentieth century.

The federal science budget 1900–14

There were also federal funds available for some scientific activities. At the beginning of the century, the federal government was spending annually an estimated $11m on science (fiscal year 1902/1903). This was a vast sum of money, equivalent to the operating budgets of the fifteen major research universities taken together. However, most of it was spent in a group of government research organisations, including the US Geological Survey, the Division of Entomology, the Bureau of Animal Industry, the Bureau of Mines, and others of a similarly directed nature. For the most part they were divorced from university science. The bureaux grew rapidly in the early part of the century, in line with their growing regulatory responsibilities.

The split between the universities' focus on basic research and the bureaux' concern with everyday matters became institutionalised.

Private research institutes

A number of research institutes were founded with private endowments in this period. They included the Rockefeller Institute for Medical Research, the Carnegie Institution and the Scripps Institution of Oceanography. For a while they bridged the gap between the universities and the government bureaux in terms of their research orientation. In the longer run they came increasingly under the influence of the universities' scientists and research preoccupations (Geiger 1986).

Industrial research

Firms in Germany in the late nineteenth century were already liaising with university laboratories (Beer 1959). It was not until much later that American universities started to develop such close research ties with industry.

The early years of the twentieth century saw the founding of the great industrial research laboratories – General Electric, Du Pont, AT&T and Eastman Kodak. These were the centres of applied, industrial research. Initially they were perceived as worlds apart from the universities.

MIT's Research Laboratory of Applied Chemistry was, in 1916, one of the first university laboratories to offer to undertake contract research for industry (Servos 1980). This initiative was not an unqualified success. There were many ups and downs over the years before MIT found a satisfactory formula for dealing with the conflicts of interest it created (see below).

The First World War and application of basic research

It was not until the First World War that industry and academe began to interact widely and effectively. The National Research Council was set up to bring together academic and industrial scientists to assist the war effort. It was outstandingly successful, leading to great advances in a wide range of technological applications including submarine detection, communications and production process technologies (Dupree 1957). The experience of this period demonstrated the practical power of science, enhancing its value in the eyes of the general public.

One outcome was that major industrialists called for a federal role in supporting basic research in universities. However, the American suspicion of central power would not permit control of the direction of science to be vested in the federal government. Thus scientific elites and private philanthropists remained the driving forces behind basic science investment until the Second World War.

The interwar period

At this time, both state-funded and private research universities saw a tremendous increase in their incomes, far outstripping the increase in student numbers. State legislatures and private philanthropists gave generously to expand and operate campus facilities. Resources were concentrated on the institutions that had already attained eminence, and now substantial amounts were being earmarked by donors for research purposes. This was particularly true of the major foundations, which decided in the 1920s to narrow the focus of their philanthropy (Geiger 1986).

By the early 1930s most of the research universities had also begun to provide funds from their general budgets specifically for research purposes. The state universities were at an advantage here, and were able to provide generous support. The private universities were well provided with endowments, but most of these were for narrowly designated purposes, or at least particular disciplines. The sums available to fill the gaps left by the terms of the endowments were usually quite modest. Cornell and Harvard both enjoyed large, general research endowments, but Stanford was able to award only $3,300. Only MIT made substantial funds (about $200,000 per annum) available from its general budget (Geiger 1986). However, during the Depression these appropriations were eventually curtailed.

The Depression

With the coming of the Depression in the 1930s the income of the great foundations was reduced. This inevitably led to a diminution of their role. The continued expansion of the university-based research effort required other sources of finance. These were not easy to find in a period of national hardship. Enrolments eventually declined, reducing fee income. Investment income from endowments fell. Most institutions went through considerable difficulties.

One compensating factor was the accompanying fall in living costs. Research students could live very cheaply. Alternative employment was not available, and the universities were able to support large numbers of temporary research workers without overspending their budgets. The effects were increasingly felt by the permanent staff of the universities. As revenues fell, the institutions eventually stopped filling vacancies. They were able to avoid actual firing by imposing salary cuts on the whole faculty. This situation lasted for several years, but towards the end of the 1930s the position eased as the economy gradually improved.

Industrial sponsorship

During the period of the universities' expansion of basic research, the great industrial laboratories had also expanded rapidly, carrying out both basic and applied research. Following the close co-operation of the First World War, the R&D-based industries retained close links with universities, supporting some contract research and consultancy work. These links were strongest in engineering and chemistry, and were of particular significance for Caltech and MIT (Geiger 1986).

A model for future funding

By the end of the 1930s the research universities were provided with excellent facilities for research and with ample, well-trained manpower. The uncertainties lay with the future provision of funding to maintain the momentum of the research enterprise. The decline of private fortunes during the Depression and the projected policies of the federal government reduced the importance of private philanthropy as a source of new funds. It became essential to find a major alternative provider of revenue.

The natural candidate was the federal government. Previously, the possibility of federal support playing a significant role in research funding had been regarded as undesirable, since it was assumed that this would undermine the principle of supporting the best science. The creation of the National Cancer Institute by Congress in 1937 was the first move to reconcile the disparate aims of the scientific elite and the federal government. Unlike the other national institutes of health, it was able to give support to researchers working within universities. It had an independent advisory board and was set up to fund the most effective research on cancer. Its mode of operation did not conflict with that of the universities, since it was designed to support the most outstanding science rather than being very narrowly goal-directed.

The Second World War and the move towards federal funding

After the start of the war, vast sums for contract research began to flow from the government to universities. This completely dominated the directions and funding of wartime research. However, it was not until 1944 that the relationship between the federal government and the universities was formalised in the report 'Science – the Endless Frontier' (Bush 1960)

This document laid down the basis for federal science policy for the postwar period. It pointed out that the progress of basic research had fallen behind that of applied research during the war.

It insisted that a relatively high ratio of basic to applied was essential to the health of the American science and technology enterprise. Since private sources could no longer sustain the growth of basic research at the prewar rate, it recommended that the federal government should play a major role through the medium of a national foundation. The guiding principles of awarding funds should be the 'best-science' criteria on which American science and technology pre-eminence had been built.

This statement laid the ground-plan for the federal strategy towards science and technology after the war. The National Science Foundation (NSF), created in 1950, was the main agency through which it was to operate.

The postwar period

In fact, the continuing growth in wealth in the USA after the Second World War led to continued generous private giving by individuals and foundations. The huge increase in federal funding dwarfed these other sources, but they enabled the universities to maintain a substantial degree of independence.

The dominance of the federal government as a source of research funding reduced the need to solicit industrial sponsorship. With the exception of a few institutions, such as MIT, prewar links with industry were eroded to a large extent.

With unrivalled facilities and ample funds for research, the American research universities were now the centre of the universe for aspiring scientists in most disciplines. The need to emulate European models had passed. They now had a self-confidence, even arrogance, in their supremacy and potency in world science.

THE FACTORS FOR RESEARCH SUCCESS

Funds

Undoubtedly the absolute abundance of support for the research universities was a major factor in the growth of American scientific pre-eminence. It was by no means the only cause. The number of different sources with differing objectives and interests helped nurture diversity within the system, and minimised the danger of any one group dominating decisions about the individuals and projects to be supported.

It should be noted again that the steady growth in research funding and scientific eminence was only experienced by a rather small number of institutions. The principle of giving to centres with established reputations consolidated their pre-eminent position. While a number of other institutions have joined them more recently, the great majority of American universities have not enjoyed advantages in any way comparable with those of the fifteen discussed here.

Objectives

The general aim of 'best science' was accepted as the criterion for funding projects, and with such a multiplex resource base this never restricted funding of novel areas. This emphasis avoided concentrating resources on pursuing highly specific goals, which while worthy might not be immediately amenable to empirical investigation. Cash was accordingly directed at projects which had a high probability of yielding results of value.

Manpower and organisation

Growing numbers of graduate students played an important part in building the science eminence and general intellectual level of the universities. They relieved faculty of part of the introductory teaching load, carried out large amounts of experimental work, and created a demand for advanced seminars.

American university departments were organised very differently from their European counterparts. The traditional European department had an all-powerful Professor who dominated every aspect of the life and work of the department. In the USA, departments could accommodate several scientists without real hierarchy. It was possible for several laboratories to coexist within a department, and junior members of staff were able to pursue independent lines of research.

The inflow of European scientists fleeing from oppression in the 1930s greatly strengthened the existing research centres. It also had a powerful cross-fertilisation effect, leading to the creation of new disciplines such as molecular biology by the 'Phage Group' (Fleming and Bailyn 1969). Europeans found the excellent facilities and organisational structures of American universities stimulating and rewarding.

It is impossible to understand fully the impact of this influx on the subsequent development of American intellectual life. Given the success achieved by many individuals in their new setting, it is probable that it was considerable. By 1969, twenty-four of these European immigrants had been awarded Nobel prizes (Geiger 1986).

Dynamism

Whatever else the research universities may have experienced, stability of funding and of expectations was not a characteristic of the interwar period. The rapid changes that were taking place were all in the direction of expansion and rising standards. They were welcomed, on the whole, and the rate of change did not lead to a loss of purpose.

THE BIOTECHNOLOGY REVOLUTION

The founding of Genentech Inc.

The period between the end of the Second World War and the early 1970s was a stable and productive era for American university-based science. Federal funding grew and a steady stream of achievements marked the period. Into this phenomenally successful and now rather inward-looking American scientific community came a new and disruptive influence, a snake in the Garden of Eden.

Genentech Inc. was formed in 1976 to develop novel drugs using recombinant DNA technology. This threw the cat among the pigeons. It brought home dramatically the realisation that much of the basic research work happening on the campus could be transformed virtually overnight into the core technologies of new companies. Molecular geneticists were still agog with the basic research implications of the powerful new technologies being developed to manipulate DNA. They were astounded to see these state-of-the-art technologies already put forward as the commercial process technologies for new products and used to raise large amounts of product development finance.

Cohen and Boyer's gene-splicing technology had only been published in 1973 (Cohen et al. 1973) and patented. Its potential was spotted by the eagle-eyed Director of Technology Transfer at

Stanford, Niels Reimers (Reimers 1987). Already Herb Boyer and venture capitalist Bob Swanson were proposing to make it the basis of a new generation of wonder drugs. Within a few years they and the new companies which followed speedily in their tracks raised hundreds of millions of dollars of equity and project finance from venture capital companies, public offerings, and corporate sponsorship. Keeping a high public profile in popular and business media, several companies have since then carried their products through ten years of development and testing to the market. Many more companies are following, currently still in the R&D stage.

Genentech, Amgen and others have transferred an entirely novel technology to the marketplace in the form of enormously profitable products. To a significant extent, the promise of these drugs has been realised, although there have been some disappointments, and they are now seen as somewhat less miraculous than was originally hoped.

The importance of generic technologies

It was speedily realised that the new, biologically based technologies had a very broad range of possible applications. They were, in fact, generic technologies – core technologies for processes in many industries.

The initial choice of the pharmaceuticals business as an entry point for the new technology was extremely shrewd. Only in such a glamorous and profitable business could the vast sums be raised that are necessary for developing novel processes and scaling up for truly commercial production. There are now many new companies with R&D projects using the same basic technologies to develop products and processes aimed at other markets. However, it is doubtful if their less strikingly exciting projects could have overcome the reluctance of large corporations and investors to embark on the risky and expensive course of funding the development of entirely new processes. Now that the initial hurdles have been overcome, the other applications of the technologies can be explored more easily.

External pressures on scientists

The development of Genentech and the other pioneers became an ongoing serial in weekly instalments for the investment community, the pharmaceutical industry and university scientists. Its publicity was skilfully orchestrated, and venture capitalists clamoured for new companies to invest in. They visited campuses looking for projects.

At the same time, one of the policies of the new companies was to keep close links with the scientific community whose continuing assistance was required to solve the problems encountered in developing the new technology. To this end, companies struggled to keep their inhouse scientists active as participants in conferences and meetings, presenting their own research alongside that of the leading university scientists. They also appointed outstanding university scientists to their 'science advisory boards'. The new company laboratories became difficult to distinguish from their university counterparts.

This kept university scientists very much in touch with the companies, which were acknowledged to be excellent places to pursue a research career. They were also lucrative places to work, and scientists usually held equity in their companies. It became common for university scientists to be offered stock in a new company in exchange for carrying out some research. They might be offered a company job to develop it further. Gradually the possibilities of becoming famous and rich while retaining scientific respectability encouraged more scientists to take the plunge. Typically in partnership with an entrepreneur, they frequently opted to set up a company themselves to exploit their own ideas.

THE EVOLUTION OF ATTITUDES

Awakening realisation in the universities

All this activity and cash flow around the biological sciences divisions of universities began to stir up interest and envy among other academics. The microelectronics companies which had grown up around Stanford and MIT had also had close links with the campuses, but they had never had this openness nor the continual public and personally lucrative participation by academic scientists.

Now those scientists who were already heavily involved with companies wanted to legitimate this within the university framework. Some of the others were keen to explore the possibilities of industrial exploitation within their own discipline. On the other hand, many were unhappy about the situation and wished to put a stop to it and its accompanying conflicts of interest.

Federal policy changes

As in the period between the two world wars, cash shortages again played a role in inducing the academic world to accept the idea of industrial sponsorship. During the 1980s, the federal government cut back severely on its funding of university non-military research. However, since the Nixon era there had been a growing awareness in government of the importance of university–industry interaction in generating innovation. Consequently legislation had been directed at encouraging joint activities.

Fiscal incentives have been put in place to encourage industrial investment in campus R&D. In 1981 the Economic Recovery Tax Act was passed, which gives a 25 per cent tax credit to increased corporate R&D. Most sponsored research in universities is covered by this. Firms are also allowed to tax-deduct much of the cost of equipment donated to universities. Co-operative programmes have been funded federally, including the NSF's 'Centers Program' (Gray *et al.* 1986a). This was set up in 1972. One of its first projects, the Polymer Processing Center at MIT, attracted continuing industrial funding and served as a prototype for later, university-based research consortia assisted by the NSF (ibid.).

The debate within the universities about how to deal with the problems that were arising was prolonged and often acrimonious. Inevitably, the universities had to accept the financial logic of the situation, albeit with mixed feelings. According to the NSF, industrial sponsorship of university research grew fourfold between 1975 and 1985, to $300m.

Continuing worries

The controversy has now died down somewhat, but some problems remain. It is still a matter for concern that university attitudes and priorities may be affected by those of companies that contribute substantially to research. Disaffectation is generated among the staff and departments which do not profit from this sponsorship.

There are fears that there may be a shift away from basic research and humanities to more commercially applied work, to the eventual detriment of all research capability. Also, inequalities between universities have increased, once again generally favouring those which are already more prosperous (Hancock 1983).

At the same time, American university attitudes have moved decisively towards the view that technology transfer is a fundamental part of the general university mission to increase the fund of human knowledge and to disseminate it as widely as possible.

POLICIES AND PRACTICE

Policy trends

The universities have adopted a pragmatic approach to resolving the problems of conflicts of interest while encouraging effective interaction with outside organisations. They have set up frameworks and policies to guide faculty and interested external parties in their joint activities.

A few universities have had successful policies of industrial liaison for a long time. The US leaders are reckoned to be Stanford and MIT. Many others are now modelling their own policies and practice on those which are associated with success in these pioneer institutions.

Technology licensing offices

Technology managers in some cases handle all aspects of industrial liaison and exploitation. In some institutions, however, particularly those with a major research commitment, the patenting and licensing functions are perceived to merit an independent organisation. The managers in these offices usually have impressive qualifications, both formal and in terms of previous experience. At least in the more successful institutions they have considerable autonomy and proper commercial budgets. Their prestige in their institutions is high, an important point for facilitating dealings with both scientists and companies.

Usually they are charged with the duty of maximising both effectiveness of exploitation of the university's IPR and the resulting revenue flow. The two goals are rather dissimilar, since most innovations lead to limited income, but they must not be neglected in favour of the occasional blockbuster which generates most of the cash (Reimers 1988). To do so would discourage inventors. In any case, royalty flow is not the only measure of the long-term value of an invention.

The cash flows at present are not great. This is partly owing to the fact that most universities have only recently started down this track. Weisbach and Burke (1990) commented in a recent review that a lapse of at least 3–5 years must be allowed before there is any expectation of profit from a university technology licensing office. They conclude that a carefully monitored patenting programme and an active licensing policy are necessary to achieve the desired results.

PATENTING AND LICENSING

General trends

Until 1980, the US federal government controlled the exploitation of intellectual property rights in patentable inventions made in the course of the research it sponsored. Government departments had different policies for dealing with this, some very restrictive. The delays and uncertainties associated with obtaining permission to exploit inventions seriously reduced the interest of both universities and companies in attempting to do so.

In an attempt to change the situation, universities demonstrated that they were more successful than the government in achieving exploitation of IPR, where they were given discretion to do so (Reimers 1988). The federal government responded, anxious to encourage technology transfer, now seen to be of key importance to economic growth. It passed Public Law 96–517 which acceded most of its rights to the universities. It retains a non-royalty bearing licence for manufacture, for governmental use only. Universities are also required to give preference to manufacturing within the USA. Inventors are guaranteed a share of the royalties. In essence, the IPR now belongs to the universities, while ensuring incentives for the inventors.

There are still problems of IPR ownership in state universities, and with industrially sponsored research. Universities are trying wherever possible to retain title to IPR, but there can be difficulties. Industrial sponsors are sometimes able to insist on ownership as a condition of contract award. State universities have to deal with claims of the state government, and also with legal complexities such as the ownership of IPR generated in the summer by an academic with a nine-month contract. The latter arrangement is common in US universities, where summer salaries are often paid by research grants, summer schools or are simply foregone.

While most American universities now actively seek to transfer their technology, they emphasise that this must be carried out with due regard to their primary institutional objectives. Their formal statements of policy to staff and to sponsors state their position on all key matters such as publication rights, commercial confidentiality, investigator's rights and responsibilities, the position of students, etc. There is significant common ground among most universities in their policies, but there are also areas in which the emphasis is very different in different institutions. The varied histories and sources of finance of the universities' activities have obviously influenced some aspects of policy.

The official statements range from a general statement, at Harvard, of the right of the academic to decide about dissemination of his research results to Columbia's positive injunction on members of staff to take ultimate moral responsibility for development and commercial exploitation of their intellectual activities (Columbia 1989).

Patent law

Patent law in most countries decrees that an invention can only be patented if there has been no public disclosure about it prior to the first patent application date. Disclosure is then permitted, and this does not affect the right to apply for patents in other centres. Foreign patents need not be applied for until a further year has elapsed.

US patent law differs from that of other countries in that disclosure is permitted for up to a year before the first patent application is filed. In certain circumstances, an additional problem may arise – inventions made in US research facilities can be accorded an invention date before the filing date of the first-filed patent application. This arises when two independent applications are made at about the same time for the same invention. In determining which is the 'first inventor', the US Patent Office only considers research activity documented in the USA (Coleman and Vandenberg 1988). This should be borne in mind when a patent application is made elsewhere and US application delayed, in the belief that the IPR is safeguarded for a year.

However, the rule on prior disclosure still precludes US inventors from applying for patent protection outside the USA. This 'enabling disclosure', or public communication, which would allow others to duplicate the invention, is not to be confused with the 'Invention Disclosure Record'.

The Invention Disclosure Record

To assist in identifying and protecting exploitable inventions, most US universities have adopted the practice of supplying all potential inventors with an 'Invention Disclosure Record'. This form is used by the scientist to record all the initial information which is required by the Technology Licensing Office to start the patenting process. It becomes part of the permanent legal record of critical facts such as the date of invention, names of inventors, description of the invention, names of other persons who know about it, etc. It is usually requested of all members of staff to submit such written records promptly.

This, in turn, should not be confused with confidential disclosure of information to companies which are potential licensees, in the course of assessing whether a new idea/invention has a market. This may be done before deciding to patent, where this might be appropriate. Again, standard forms of agreement to honour confidentiality and intellectual property of the institution are often employed.

Some features of licensing agreements

Most American universities claim that it is their policy to license primarily 'for the public good'. In the early days this usually meant a non-exclusive licence, supposedly to encourage the widest possible use of the invention. But experience showed that without at least some exclusivity, companies were unwilling to undertake the development expense. Now most institutions will award exclusive licences.

Most inventions have not been tested extensively for their usefulness. This would incur costs which institutions are usually unwilling to shoulder. As a condition of most licences, the university usually disclaims all responsibility for the invention, either for its effectiveness in its possible uses or for any possible harm it might do, for example, side effects of drugs. This is of particular importance in the litigious climate of the USA. This disclaimer is usually accompanied by a specific condition that licensees will cover the costs of liability actions, and meet any requirements for liability insurance cover.

Licences may cover subsequent 'improvements' on the original invention but this is not favoured. It can cause difficulties for continuity of university research funding and conflict with other contractual claims since it may involve work sponsored from another source. Consequently, 'improvements' are often specifically excluded from the licence.

There are other common features of licensing agreements, mostly designed to give maximal encouragement to licensees to exploit the invention speedily and effectively. They include due diligence clauses and annual payments to be made in the absence of royalty income. Johns Hopkins, for instance, retains the right to terminate the licensing agreement after two years if no commercial sales have been made. In addition, a minimum royalty payment must be made for these two years.

The IPR and any ensuing royalty income are often assigned to a wholly owned subsidiary of the university. This serves to distance the university and its procedures from the technology transfer function. There are a number of reasons why this might be advantageous, not least of which is the further distancing of the university and its endowment from liability for the invention.

Royalties are ultimately divided in slightly different ways, depending on the institution. Many allow a higher percentage to go to the inventor when total sums are small. After deduction of costs, inventors usually receive 25–50 per cent of the residue. The university may take the rest into general funds, or divide it with the department or school.

Technology transfer organisations

It is increasingly acknowledged that the most difficult step in innovation is the transition from the university laboratory to the company's systems (Nelsen 1988a). Two approaches are currently regarded as beneficial in assisting this process.

One is to set up a small R&D company on or near the campus to develop the invention. This is most commonly done where there is no industrial sponsor wishing to exercise its option to exploit. Occasionally, however, a sponsor will choose to set up a wholly owned subsidiary or joint venture company on campus as a vehicle for the early development stage. The company-formation route to innovation will be discussed further in a later chapter.

The other approach is to carry out early development work in a purpose-built 'technology transfer organisation' on campus which is designed specifically to permit the continuing interaction between university and company staff required by the early transfer processes. The aim is to create an environment that facilitates cooperative work between academic scientists and company personnel so that the invention can be carried through the early stages of commercialisation.

These organisations are sometimes set up by the institution alone, or together with one or more industrial sponsors and other interested parties. This has been encouraged by changes in US antitrust legislation which make it easier for companies to engage in collaborative R&D.

In the early 1980s there were a number of such organisations set up to develop microelectronics technology. Anxious to keep close to the sources of invention, many microelectronics companies formed university/industry collaborative research centres. The largest is the Microelectronics and Computer Technology Corporation (MCC), on the Austin campus of the University of Texas. It is supported by twenty-one major US microelectronics firms, which were contributing $75m per year in 1986 (Rogers 1986), and by the US Defense Department. In 1986 a total of twenty-five microelectronics centres had been set up on other campuses including Stanford, Arizona State and MIT (ibid.).

The next major group to be set up was the biotechnology centres. Cornell's Biotechnology Transfer Project started in 1986 and its Biotechnology Institute is a joint project supported by Cornell, Eastman Kodak, General Foods and Rhone-Poulenc. The University of Kansas set up the Higuchi Biosciences Center, working in partnership with industry and the Kansas Technology Enterprise Corporation, to exploit its strength in bioanalytical chemistry. In Baltimore, the University of Maryland's Biotechnology Institute has set up a number of organisations including the Center of Marine Biotechnology, each focusing on particular local strengths which currently generate strong commercial interest. Similar organisations have been set up on many campuses and science parks.

The federal government has also played a part. Between 1980 and

1985 the NSF established twenty-nine centres along the lines of the MIT Polymer Processing Center (see above). Usually they had funding of $250,000–$600,000 over five years. By 1986 six had become self-funding (Gray *et al.* 1986a). This success prompted the NSF to commit further funds for engineering research centres (ibid.). The centres were novel in involving consortia and were often interdisciplinary. There was industrial participation in recommending and evaluating projects. At the same time, ultimate authority regarding operations remained with the university.

There appear to be several factors which facilitate success in the centres. Only universities doing a significant amount of R&D can attract industrial partners. The goals must be agreed by participants, and the most important must be the expansion of general knowledge, rather than the pursuit of patents. The programme of research must be diverse and interdisciplinary. New research linkages must be created. A strong leader and good formal communications systems are essential for achievement of the goals set (Gray *et al.*1986a).

POLICIES AND PRACTICE OF SEVERAL MAJOR INSTITUTIONS

Stanford

Stanford was one of the pioneers of technology transfer. This is thanks, in great measure, to Frederick Terman (Reimers 1988), who created Stanford Industrial Park on the campus when he was Dean of Engineering. There were few employment opportunities for Stanford graduates in the surrounding idyllic farmland. Terman, later Provost of Stanford University, felt that the university should encourage the exploitation of its technology locally, to fill this gap.

Encouraged by him, two of his former students, David Packard and William Hewlett set up in business on the industrial park. The story of Hewlett-Packard's rise to international success and fortune as a major electronics company has become a textbook classic.

Terman also set up Stanford Research Institute, which was intended to interface between the university and industry. In 1971 it became independent and is now called SRI International. Among more recent initiatives is Stanford's Center for Integrated Systems

(CIS), a research consortium opened in 1981, which received $15m from twenty US microelectronics firms and $15m from the US Department of Defense.

Stanford also has an Industry Affiliate Programme – subscribing companies receive early copies of publications, have early access to graduate students, and are invited to participate in an annual symposium. This is a relatively informal way of encouraging regular interaction.

Patenting and licensing

The Stanford Office of Technology Licensing specifically handles patenting and licensing. It does not involve itself in faculty consultancy or research contracts, which have a separate office. In 1988 the office had sixteen employees, of whom ten were trained initially as scientists or engineers. The highest priority is set on good marketing (Reimers 1988). Thus personnel must have first, good communication skills; second, good deal-making and financial skills; and third, good technical understanding. In 1987, revenue was about $9m. The cost of operation for the year was in the region of $1m.

The last Director, Niels Reimers, who patented the Boyer-Cohen gene-splicing technology, comments (Reimers 1988) that most inventions have a restricted, niche market which is easy to identify. The major money-spinners are rare, and usually costly to develop in terms of time and cash. In the case of the gene-splicing patent, open licences are offered with royalty rates depending on the degree of importance the technology has in the product as a whole (Reimers 1987).

Royalties

Royalties received by Stanford are divided as follows: 15 per cent deducted for office costs, then the residue is divided equally between the inventor, the department and the school.

MIT

MIT first formally undertook to provide contract research services for industry in 1916, with the founding of its Research Laboratory of Applied Chemistry. It extended its commitment to industrial liaison in 1919. This was the year when it initiated its Technology Plan; at this time it was suffering from a shortfall in endowment funding. It was decided to secure corporate donations by offering special services for five years, in return. These included use of its library, and preferred access to its alumni and students, for recruitment. The plan was extremely successful (MIT Treasurer's Report 1919) in its first round. When the university offered to renew it for a further five years, there was no interest among clients (Geiger 1986). However, industrially supported research funding for projects across a wide range of disciplines grew steadily. It would appear that the initial plan was too vague for such disparate partners: expectations on both sides went unfulfilled. No doubt the experience contributed towards MIT's current strong preference for straightforward published policies and standard contracts.

In these early days, difficulties had already arisen prefiguring the debates of the late 1970s, when contractual secrecy requirements conflicted with the academic's desire to publish (Servos 1980). There was also dissatisfaction among MIT academics at the level of their salaries compared with those of the industrial colleagues with whom they were in close contact. Many preferred to supplement their incomes by consulting rather than to spend time on research. The uneasy compromises reached led to widespread unhappiness among the faculty. The institute's reputation suffered.

In 1930 a new President was appointed, Karl T. Compton. His remit was to rescue the institute's reputation by developing a strong basic science research function (Killian 1985). He addressed the problems with great effect. Announcing the new emphasis on research and teaching in the fundamental sciences, he managed to raise substantial funds from the Rockefeller Foundation. He centralised industrial liaison and developed formal policies about the role of consultancy and industrial sponsorship in the university. He also addressed the problems of secrecy, patenting and overhead charges, three areas of key importance to this day. It became a matter of policy that only research and consultancy that addressed important topics and demanded the highest levels of competence would be undertaken.

By the end of the 1930s, MIT's position as one of the great research universities was reinstated. Its commitment to industrial liaison and technology transfer has continued, its effectiveness bolstered by a clear, well-disseminated policy and very effectiveenabling structures. This minimises conflicts of interest, and when they do arise, there are procedures for adjudication.

Today's policies

MIT's policy documents and its standard licensing forms are all clearly written, well-indexed documents (MIT 1988). They are backed up by explanatory articles written by executives in the Licensing Office which explain and clarify points that are often misunderstood.

The main thrust of the policy is that technology transfer, while important, remains secondary to education and research. Free dissemination of information must be minimally delayed. Staff are advised that they should notify the Technology Licensing Office of an idea or invention which they think might have commercial possibilities. Tight time limits are specified within which the institute must decide whether to patent an invention, and to make the application. A few weeks after notification, the scientist is free to publish, if he chooses. Often the decision to patent is made in consultation with an industrial sponsor, but MIT almost always retains the IPR, regardless of sponsorship.

MIT will only accept research funding from one of its licensees under precisely defined conditions.

Licensing

MIT will license to its own staff or students, where there is no conflict of interest or commitment. MIT will sometimes accept an equity share in a company in lieu of cash royalties.

It encourages support and co-operation of the inventor in development of the invention, seeing this as crucial to success (Nelsen 1988b).

Royalties

Fifteen per cent of gross royalty income is deducted to cover the expenses of the Technology Licensing Office, then costs directly assignable to the specific case (such as patent filing, etc.) are deducted. Of the remainder, one-third goes to the inventor(s) and the rest is divided between the MIT General Fund and the department. This also applies to students and to visitors who are inventors (MIT 1988).

Harvard

Harvard, always the best-endowed of the private research universities, used its abundant cash to create an excellent research environment. It paid high salaries and its facilities were uniformly excellent. However, its reluctance under Lawrence Lowell's presidency to appoint any but its own PhDs during the 1920s and early 1930s gradually eroded its high standing.

The appointment of Conant as President in 1933 initiated an era in which individual achievement was the only measure considered in making appointments. It became a matter of routine to have all promotions vetted by independent committees, including non-Harvard specialists (Geiger 1986).

Research funds

Harvard never lacked for research funding, particularly for medical research. By 1930 it had nearly 1,000 earmarked research funds.

It has recently formalised its policy on technology transfer but this is still rather unclear. In 1986 it declared a policy aim that the greatest possible public benefit should accrue (Harvard 1986). Its November 1987 'Guide to patents' affirms the right of faculty members to disseminate information as they please, and states that Harvard sees its role as providing the means to patent, for those who choose to do so (Harvard 1987). This is a very different attitiude from that of most other US universities, which are very insistent on their ownership of IPR and the faculty's duty to notify any patentable invention. Harvard does require notification, but it is not obvious how this relates to the rest of its policy. It is only strongly concerned to retain IPR in the case of medical inventions. Where it is not precluded in the contract with a sponsor, the inventor in many cases has first option to apply for the patent and to retain royalties. Where the university has supported the work, it expects a share in the returns.

Royalties

Where the university has taken title to IPR, royalties are divided as follows: net income of up to $50,000 is distributed with 35(25) per cent going to the inventor, 30(40) per cent to the department, 20 per cent to the faculty and 15 per cent to the university. The bracketed figures show the shareout when net income exceeds $50,000 (Harvard 1988).

Gifts to Harvard from successful inventors are appreciated.

Cornell University

Cornell University regards technology transfer very much as a part of its primary mission. Founded as a land grant college, its historical orientation has always favoured a strong commitment to the economic welfare of the New York State community (Cornell 1986).

Its technology transfer is handled by the Cornell Research Foundation Inc., a wholly owned, non-profit subsidiary of Cornell University. It holds IPR assignable to Cornell. Its purpose is to transfer IPR for the benefit of the public, while using the income as an incentive for creativity (Cornell 1989a). Cornell has standard contract documents and policies. However, it favours a flexible approach, provided that goals are well defined, the body of technology is precisely delimited, and future projects are not prejudiced.

H. Walter Haeussler, the Director of Patents and Technology Marketing, remarks that it is essential to state formally a position of willingness to embark on joint development of new technology, by making a statement about the sorts of agreements which are acceptable. This encourages venture capitalists and other entrepreneurial groups to interact with university development organisations and inventors. Having established an interest, the parties will then enquire about the possibility of negotiating terms agreeable to everyone. Without a statement of some sort, outsiders will not ask (Haeussler 1987).

This is a very interesting point of view, worth considering by those UK Directors of Industrial Liaison who are so anxious to adapt contracts to suit each individual case, that they will not put anything in writing before the start of negotiations.

Some of the main features of Cornell's standard research contract and licensing agreements are as follows. Research contracts preserve the absolute right to publish, with a total of 120 days' delay in which the sponsor can review a proposed publication and file a patent application. Unless the inventor agrees, there is no possible further delay. This is non-negotiable.

Licensing

Cornell's standard contract with sponsors of research promises that where IPR is generated, the sponsor will get at least as good a licensing agreement as any other organisation, but without a guarantee of exclusivity. Options agreements are used to allow a potential licensee to examine new ideas, in strictest confidence, before making a final decision to license.

The licensing objective is to incentivise new product investment. The terms are set in accordance with this. Licences are only exclusive where this is justified. Where an exclusive licence is granted, there is a minimum annual fee to encourage exploitation. Royalties are quite high as an incentive to earn. Failure of a licensee to make reasonable efforts to commercialise an invention is a breach of the agreement, as is any failure to maintain quality control and observation of legal requirements.

A licensee must pay all foreign licence filing and maintenance fees. Prosecution of a third party for infringement of the patent is at the discretion of the Foundation. If it elects not to prosecute, the licensee may do so and may defray expenses to the extent of 50 per cent of royalties payable during the lawsuit. The Foundation can recover this sum out of any damages awarded. Cornell requires that it carry no liability associated with the commerciality of technology. Licensees carry all business risk. No warranties are given. Sub-licensing is not automatically allowed, but may be permitted with the Foundation's approval of the sub-licensee.

An arbitration procedure is laid down for dealing with disputes, with the State Court as a last resort.

Royalties

CRF Inc. deducts all costs from gross royalties, then a 15 per cent management fee. The remaining royalties are divided between the inventor(s) and the division of the university to which he or she belongs, according to a sliding scale from 50:50 to 15:85, as total royalties rise (Cornell 1989b).

Direct involvement

Cornell has a Business and Technology Park and involves itself in technology transfer organisations and start-up companies. This will be discussed in more detail in Chapter 6.

Rockefeller University

Founded in 1901 with an endowment of $65m, Rockefeller was initially a pure medical research institute modelled on European organisations such as the Pasteur Institute in Paris. In the 1950s it reorganised itself into a university for graduate training and research, in medicine and the biological sciences.

Its primary mission is to carry out fundamental scientific investigations for the good of mankind (Rockefeller 1985). Its research projects are initiated by investigators, not sponsors. It still maintains a rather more arms-length attitude to sponsors than MIT, Cornell or Stanford.

Research contracts

Research contracts require the sponsor to specify its objectives. The aim is to enhance awareness of possible applications. Sponsors are expected to top up research funding with an appropriate level of unrestricted funding for use in maintenance of university core components such as libraries, etc.

The university reviews sponsored research projects annually. Audits of the research, administration and financial procedures are carried out. Peer review at longer intervals is suggested. Sponsored research frequently carries contractual rights of first refusal by the sponsor.

Licensing

Rockefeller has a positive policy of licensing its technologies where it judges they will do most good. It is committed to the effective use of knowledge. It will actively search for licensees where no commitment to sponsors exists. Both exclusive and non-exclusive arrangements are entered into (Rockefeller 1986).

HOW SUCCESSFUL?

How effective are these arrangements for technology transfer? It is very difficult to assess this, and indeed few exercises in evaluation have been undertaken. Attempts have been made to measure the results of the NSF Centers Program (Gray *et al.* 1986a). They have demonstrated its success in terms of the continuing interest of participants and the fact that several are now self-funding. The extent to which they have fostered innovation has not yet been assessed.

A recent study (Mansfield 1991) looked at products and processes commercialised between 1975 and 1985 in seventy-six major US companies across a range of industries. According to executives of the companies, 11 per cent of products and 9 per cent of processes had depended on academic research, carried out 7 years before commercialisation, on average. The percentage in the high technology industries, particularly pharmaceuticals and information processing, was much higher. Unfortunately, this research only covers the earlier part of the current period of industry/ university liaison.

The early initiatives achieved results sufficiently desirable that they have been used as a model for many of the more recent ventures. But in the long run, will the ambitious new schemes be seen as equally successful? Some of them are already winning approval as valuable interfaces between the academic and company worlds. Semiconductor companies in California have indicated that they are getting what they want from collaborative centres, namely a useful mode of introduction to future employees and academic consultants (Larsen 1984).

However, Eveland's (1985) analysis of communications between individuals in nine collaborative R&D centres assisted by the NSF underlines the fact that very little communication will take place between industry and university representatives unless they are in close, physical proximity. This emphasises the need to plan these centres carefully, if they are to be in any degree effective. This was further confirmed in Mansfield's (1991) study, which found a high and very effective level of technology transfer between a large number of major American companies and universities which were in close physical proximity to company laboratories.

The more tangible spin-off – thriving high technology companies in the vicinity; large corporations queuing up to set up their own

R&D nearby; a general boost to the local economy – may take a long time, as in the case of the Research Triangle in North Carolina which took twenty years to get going. A recent study (Redwood *et al.* 1989) of more than 300 Kansas firms showed a substantial level of awareness of and interest in the services that local universities could offer. However, this was accompanied by severe difficulties in accessing these resources. Major problems of locating appropriate expertise and of achieving effective communication were reported. These are soluble problems, but time and patient bridge-building activities are required.

Chapter 4

Technology transfer from UK research organisations

British scientists in the nineteenth century were largely ignored by both the state and industry (Turner 1980). The little state funding they received was channelled mainly through the army and navy (Brock 1890). By 1868 fears were already being voiced of the German industrial threat (Cardwell 1957). Thomas H. Huxley's famous letter to *The Times* on 20 January 1887 called for Britain to prepare for victory in the industrial war. The indifference of political parties of the day led to considerable disillusion among scientists with the political system. Their unsuccessful encounters with politicians and civil servants trained in the classics led many scientists to deplore the requirement for Greek for entrance to the ancient universities (Armstrong 1910).

In spite of these early difficulties, science and technology gradually attained a significant level of public support in Britain. The inadequacy of scientific resources in Britain during the First World War led to the creation of a separate government department, the Department of Scientific and Industrial Research (DSIR) in 1916 (Bernal 1939). This was the main source of scientific support for the next fifty years. Between the wars, virtually all its efforts went into encouraging industrial research and into setting up applied research institutes. Its support of university research was non-existent. The Medical Research Council, established in 1920, set up a small number of applied research establishments, but most of its funds went to smaller research groups based in universities. This was the modest start of government research support for university-based science. The Agricultural Research Council, established in 1931, also chose to maintain a few, university-based groups.

The level of government expenditure on research grew steadily, but it was the outbreak of the Second World War which led to substantial public expenditure on the science base. As Stafford Cripps said in 1941, 'This was going to be a truly scientific war'. As in the USA, UK science and technology policy after the Second World War was heavily influenced by the successful marriage of scientific and technical resources during the war itself. The initial emphasis was strongly on military technology (Freeman 1986; Salomon 1973). This broadened in the 1960s and 1970s to embrace a more general concern with the need for technical change. At the same time there was a growing realisation of the need for a more cost-effective approach. The allocation of huge amounts of public money to prestige projects was questioned (Henderson 1977).

THE FAILURE OF UK INNOVATION

For many years now it has been a source of concern that while British science is still outstandingly inventive, British technology-based industry – with a few notable exceptions – has a poor record of success in introducing new products and processes. Somewhere in the chain of innovation from the first idea to the finished product or process there are missing links (see Chapter 7).

The origins of the biotechnology revolution in American university laboratories, coming on the heels of the microelectronics revolution which had only slightly weaker campus links, excited considerable interest in the UK in the late 1970s. Britain has an outstanding record in bioscience research, with a string of Nobel prizes to its credit. Much of the work underpinning the new technologies was carried out with public sponsorship in UK laboratories, including the development of monoclonal antibodies (Kohler and Milstein 1975). This was one of the two key breakthroughs that underpin commercial biotechnology. It is a process for mass-production of biosensor molecules with extraordinary powers to detect target substances precisely at very low concentration. It is now the basis of several major businesses: much of the diagnostics business, purification processes, some novel drugs, drug delivery vehicles, and many other products.

At the time of the discovery, Milstein, suspecting that there might be industrial applications, informed the National Research and Development Corporation, the UK government body which at that time had responsibility for exploitation of publicly funded inventions. The NRDC failed to see the potential of the discovery and did not patent it. This was subsequently seized on as incontrovertible evidence of the inadequacy of the existing technology transfer mechanisms. It was held to exemplify one of the root causes of the decline of British industry – failure to recognise, protect and transfer novel technologies from British laboratories to British industry.

American success

The conspicuous success with which new American companies were taking technology from the frontiers of academic research into ambitious product development projects was held up as a model. These companies, with their close campus contacts, were attracting contract and equity finance from large corporations, venture capitalists and other investors. How could the UK emulate this dynamic progress? There was widespread debate about the factors which had fostered the phenomenon. Government was called upon to intervene.

At about the same date, awareness was beginning to develop in the UK as elsewhere that another great period of radical technological change had begun. From the late 1970s the steady convergence of computing and communications technologies on the one hand, and the perceived potential of bioscience-based technologies on the other have focused attention on the growing importance of these novel generic technologies. Under the labels of IT (Information Technology) and Biotechnology they have stimulated a continuing debate in all the major industrial nations and trading blocs. The heart of the debate has been about what measures should be taken nationally to maintain competitiveness in these technologies, and what role international co-operation should play.

All these concerns have come together, as the perception has grown that solutions to any of the problems must address all of them. Feelings of urgency crystallised in the west in 1981, when the Japanese announced their Fifth Generation Project (Arnold and Guy 1986). This event catalysed the formation of a number of major, government-led electronics and computer technology development programmes in the USA and Europe, as well as supranational efforts in the EC, many of which are still in progress, or in phase II or III. Over the same period, in most of these countries, policy-makers have tried to achieve general improvement in the quality of university/business/government interaction.

UK GOVERNMENT ATTEMPTS TO IMPROVE THE
UNIVERSITY SUPPLY SIDE

In 1977, acknowledging the lack of interaction between industry and academe in the UK, the Under-Secretary of State at the Department of Industry stated as a matter of policy that university research expertise should in future be brought together with the skills of industry (Academic Industrial Collaboration 1977). It was recognised that there were obstacles to co-operation, including the inadequate information flow between universities and industry, but ideas on how to improve the situation were limited. The absence of incentives for academics and industry to get together was not mentioned.

After the Conservatives were returned to power in 1979, the policy changed markedly. Predictably, the Thatcher government declined to respond with significant direct intervention, preferring to open up the existing government monopoly over technology transfer to competition. Universities were strongly encouraged to meet the needs of industry more closely and to attract more private sector finance in the process (DES 1985).

The importance of the reward system has been recognised and some features have been improved. The inventing institutions have been offered an incentive by giving them the responsibilities and rewards of exploiting their own inventions. On the whole they pass on a fair proportion of any financial rewards to the inventors, but their success in this respect does not yet lead to improved career opportunities within academia.

The importance of encouraging new company formation has also been recognised. The Thatcher government set as an objective the improvement of the business environment for smaller companies. It took several initiatives designed to achieve this end, such as creating the Unlisted Securities Market, measures to reduce the burden of bureaucracy on small companies, etc. There have also been some joint university/industry research initiatives, designed to address perceived gaps in technological capacity. The effectiveness of these measures is discussed below.

While offering the carrot of technology licensing income to the universities, the government also wielded the stick. The growth of public expenditure on higher education and research has been curtailed. This has forced universities to look for alternative sources of general income and research support. They have been strongly encouraged by government to offer their varied expertise on a commercial basis to industry and the community, in addition to carrying out their traditional teaching and research activities.

Before this period, only a few institutions had any formal policy or organisation for dealing with this function. Now nearly all have at least one executive and usually a whole office of industrial liaison designated to interface with industrial and other clients (Bower 1992).

Case study: Heriot-Watt University's Department of Building Engineering and Surveying

University departments often include individuals involved in activities as disparate as teaching, basic research, contract research, industrial consultancy and government policy-making. The array of expertise and contacts brought together in a single commonroom offers unique possibilities for cross-communication.

In the case of Heriot-Watt's Department of Building, members of staff are active in all these areas, carrying out basic research in material science; some on contract testing work; consulting on, for example, 'sick building syndrome'; sitting on international committees deciding building standards; and so on. Two members of staff have managed to find the time to start companies of their own – Arcaid and Panorama – which offer a multimedia property database management system. Companies interacting with the department are able to tap the resources of this unusual combination of skills and information.

Until recently, few university departments realised the nature of their own in-house expertise. This is changing now, and with greater self-awareness is coming a much greater understanding of what they have to offer which will be useful to other organisations.

UNIVERSITY/INDUSTRY JOINT PROJECTS: GOVERNMENT INITIATIVES

For most academics the idea of collaborating with industrial partners on a directed programme of research was very different to anything in their previous experience. For a substantial number it was not even regarded as a legitimate mode of operation. This was recognised in the mid-1970s at the Science Research Council, later to become the Science and Engineering Research Council (SERC).

The SRC had been mainly concerned until this point with funding research proposals initiated by academics. Now a need was felt for an additional proactive function.

It proposed the establishment of special units within the SRC charged with the responsibility of setting up and managing strategically focused programmes of research and training in partnership with industry. This led to the creation of the directorate system, in which a Director, an outstanding scientist with industrial experience, was responsible for investigating industrial needs and locating appropriate research expertise within the universities. The directorate would then commission and co-ordinate a programme of research to meet those needs, and to generate a suitable pool of trained manpower. The first such programme was set up in 1976 in polymer engineering. This was followed by a series of programmes directed towards different technological areas.

The DCS programme

It was perceived that, even where academic scientists and industry were willing, there was usually little knowledge of what they might have to offer each other, and less of how to arrange and manage a collaborative project. The SRC decided in 1976 to establish the Distributed Computing Systems Programme to co-ordinate a programme of research on information technology (Duce 1984).

Individual scientists were organised into a communicating group. Industrial relevance was a criterion for support. Industry was linked in, but in an advisory rather than an active role. Industrial members were on the panel and were invited to workshops. There were hopes that technology would be transferred (Oakley and Owen 1989). The DCS programme ended in 1984, but some of the projects it had funded were carried on into the Alvey Programme (see below).

Project Universe

Project Universe (UNIVersity Expanded Ring and Satellite Experiment) was the next major step, linking computer and communications technologies. It was originally proposed to the SRC as a three-year project linking three university teams and a group at the SRC's Rutherford Appleton Laboratory. It planned to study the possibility of connecting local computer area networks by satellite to form a high-speed, wide-area network. The SRC was favourably disposed, but felt a number of other participants should be involved, including industrial partners who could help to fund the commercially relevant work.

In 1981 the plan was approved, with British Telecom, GEC and Logica participating. They contributed substantially towards the costs, assisted to a maximum of 50 per cent by the Department of Trade and Industry (DTI). This was the first truly collaborative programme involving university, industry and government partners. It was reckoned to be reasonably successful by all the groups involved and became a model for later projects of this type (Oakley and Owen 1989).

The fifth generation – Alvey

At about the same time, a British government team was sent to Japan to an international meeting concerning possible objectives for a 'fifth-generation' computer research and development programme. The powerful Japanese Ministry for International Trade and Industry (MITI) was keen to enlist western expertise in a joint programme. Returning from the meeting, the team warned of the wary response of other nations to the Japanese proposals for collaboration. On the other hand, they suggested that the Japanese plans could be taken as a model for any country's efforts to organise its development of IT resources. They strongly recommended that Britain should rapidly concentrate financial and other resources on promoting key technologies in key sectors. Unsurprisingly, they were opposed to any extensive research collaboration with Japan until such time as Britain had improved its own ability to exploit the results.

This view was confirmed by senior scientists and officials, and in 1982 John Alvey, a Senior Director for Technology at British Telecom, was invited by the government to chair a group whose remit was to plan a research programme on IT. The group drew up a broad plan for developing four enabling technologies: Intelligent Knowledge-Based Systems (IKBS); Very Large-Scale Integration (VLSI); software engineering and Man/Machine Interfaces (MMI). It was reckoned that major advances in all these areas would be required, and that one of the strategic objectives should be to make the UK a world leader in software technology by the end of the decade. It was also suggested that a UK-based programme would help UK companies to participate more effectively in the European Community's proposed ESPRIT programme (see Chapter 6).

The breadth of the proposed programme, and the desire for a high level of industrial funding led to questions about how tight central direction of the programme could be. Large companies wanted to control the project and subcontract parts to other companies and universities. Other groups wanted to involve many companies and a broader range of research. The idea of centring the programme around an institute was rejected in favour of linking groups by an electronic network.

After the Alvey Report was published in 1982, industry and other groups were asked to comment. The main thrust was accepted, and the Alvey Programme was finally set up in 1983 with a total budget of £350m over five years, of which 50 per cent was to come from public sources. A small directorate was set up within the DoI to manage the programme, and Brian Oakley, the Secretary of the SERC, was appointed Director. The MoD and SRC were also closely involved.

Constitution

The Alvey Programme was organised very differently from previous British technology support programmes (Arnold and Guy 1986). It was interdisciplinary in the widest sense, involving groups from many different academic and industrial backgrounds, and from three different arms of government. There were a total of 210 co-operative projects, each involving two or three firms and one or two universities. Fifty of the firms were small – fewer than 400 employees. Most universities, many polytechnics and several public sector research institutes were involved. Within a short period this led to greatly increased willingness of academics to call up colleagues in industry and vice versa (Oakley and Owen 1989). A cultural change appeared to be taking place.

Management

Such an ambitious and novel project inevitably posed novel administrative problems. The solutions employed were not always satisfactory and there were delays in implementation. As described by Oakley, the management of the programme had some key differences from its precursors, starting with the initial stages of project design. Instead of having formal dates for submission of proposals, the consortia preparing the proposals were encouraged to discuss the developing proposals with the directorate throughout the preparation period. This was not liked by the participants (PREST/SPRU 1987), but it allowed greater co-ordination of project coverage. Another major innovation was that the assessment of proposals, in addition to the traditional criteria, included consideration of factors that would facilitate co-operation and exploitation.

These last were the most difficult to assess (Oakley and Owen 1989). This was not because academics were reluctant to think about exploitation – on the contrary, Oakley reports that in most cases they were fully as eager as the industrial scientists. The problem was rather to choose between projects that might have had widespread application in industry and those that had a more restricted application, partly due to higher capital costs, but which were strongly supported by a major company. Assurances of future exploitation from large companies sometimes overcame the directorate's preference for less capital-demanding projects. However, with hindsight, Oakley remarks that the companies themselves ultimately proved unwilling to make the large capital investment necessary to implement some of the successful projects commercially.

Another management problem was communications. The electronic network was ultimately used by few of the projects. The most successful medium of communication was 'Alvey News', a traditional free newsletter. Alvey conferences also proved to be an effective way of keeping the community together.

Monitoring and evaluation

Procedures for monitoring were not put in place until the projects were underway. Each project had its own independent monitoring officer who reported regularly to the directorate.

The directorate also appointed two academic teams to evaluate the programme jointly. Their interim report (PREST/SPRU 1987) noted that Alvey had improved existing links, rather than creating new ones. It found that the programme had been fairly successful in the intangible areas of creating technological awareness, facilitating future collaboration and developing a research community. On the negative side, management and information systems were criticised and it was pointed out that much of the research needed follow-up work to reach the stage of exploitability.

This report was criticised on the grounds of excessive academicism. No independent commercial organisation contributed to the evaluation. However, the programme was also subjected to a critical evaluation by the National Audit Office: this attacked several aspects (NAO 1988). It found major administrative weaknesses, some due to the delays in installing management and information systems which were noted in the PREST/SPRU report. It also found that the rate of exploitation of the research was below the Alvey Committee's own expectation. It suggested that the directorate could have been more proactive in securing speedy exploitation. While it agreed that substantial co-operation had been generated between academia and industry, it found that large firms dominated projects, and participants complained about lack of support from the directorate. In fact, the NAO report did not differ in any major respect from the PREST/SPRU report. Unfortunately, no private sector report was commissioned.

In a final report from the PREST/SPRU teams (Guy *et al.* 1991), the point was made again that academic/industrial collaboration was successful, and also that the academic ability to understand industrial perspectives improved in the course of the programme. This suggests that Alvey has at least improved the environment for co-operation between academia and industry. However, the report deplored the failure of participant companies to make use of the outcomes of the projects. This points up the same key problem of European companies noted in a study carried out by the European Industrial Research Managers' Association (EIRMA 1986), i.e. the failure to integrate research and development activities into the mainstream of company strategic planning processes.

The Biotechnology Directorate

British basic biological research has been highly regarded internationally for a long time. The British chemical and pharmaceutical industries are among the few technology-based industries in which Britain is still indisputably an important international player. It was perceived that the wide range of subject disciplines involved in university research relevant to biotechnology had not yet formed a grouping which could be easily recognised by industry. Thus it is not surprising that the emerging bioscience-based technologies, whose novel process technologies are crucial to the further development of chemistry-based technologies, have also been the subject of a public sector programme. The Biotechnology Directorate was established in 1981. It has been reviewed favourably twice, and continues to operate.

Its original remit was to identify research priorities, to formulate and co-ordinate an interdisciplinary research programme, and to create a national biotechnology community. Industrial and academic participants were to be involved, and exploitation promoted. An SRC-based directorate was set up to manage the programme. The government was reluctant to provide special funding for this programme, on the grounds that both the science and the private sector were doing very well without such assistance. Thus its budget was made up largely from funds already earmarked within the SRC for research in the relevant areas. The sums involved have been small compared with the Alvey Programme, from just over £1m in 1982/83 to just over £4m in 1988/89 (Senker and Sharp 1988).

This has created tension between the SRC (now SERC) and the Medical Research Council (MRC), which has traditionally funded much of the research in the areas designated by the directorate as high priority. British science has made major contributions to the new bioscience-based technologies now being successfully commercialised mainly in the USA. In several cases these have been recognised by the award of Nobel prizes. Virtually all of this work, however, has been funded by the MRC, often within its own research units.

The MRC has perceived the directorate as a potential competitor for funds and for prestige. Consequently it has refused to co-operate in the Biotechnology Directorate's projects (Senker and Sharp 1988). On the other hand, its own attempts at commercialisation have not been particularly successful, and it has not been seen as a more appropriate home for the directorate.

In spite of its modest means and the rivalries which limited participation in its projects, the directorate's effectiveness in interfacing companies and academics through a series of clubs and workshops has been commended. It has also been credited with success in raising the profile of biotechnology. However, the number of firms involved remains small; as with Alvey, large companies dominate to the detriment of smaller firms (ibid.).

Other programmes

The DTI has set up a number of smaller programmes to assist in industry/academic collaboration. These include the Teaching Company Scheme, involving academics in a long-term consultancy relationship with an individual company, and the Link Scheme, which supports research collaboration between companies and university scientists over a wide range of technological areas.

Britain also participates in a number of major international research programmes underpinning technological competitiveness. These include all the EC R&D programmes and also the American Strategic Defense Initiative. This last involvement has not been very extensive, and it is unclear what benefits might accrue to British industry (Arnold and Guy 1986).

RECENT GOVERNMENT INITIATIVES

In 1988 the DTI published a White Paper promising a greater emphasis on technology transfer, especially between educational institutions and industry (DTI 1989). The need to make better use of academic resources is specifically recognised; assisting the diffusion of important new technologies is a major aim.

Now (1991) these policies are being implemented, and a number of new programmes are beginning. Most of these are targeted at smaller companies, offering consultancy services and financial support. The emphasis has moved away from large-scale projects under MoD or DTI control, with large companies as the main partners (Arnold and Guy 1986).

Less attention appears to have been given to the academic side of the transfer equation. There are no obvious indications that the government has perceived a need to offer more encouragement to the academics whom it expects to participate in these activities. Thus it has not yet addressed the fact that academic career advancement is still very much tied to rate of publication in academic journals, with no rewards for the industrial involvement which the government is apparently eager to encourage.

A spokesman for the Committee of Vice Chancellors and Principals recently indicated that the CVCP is very aware of this anomaly (THES 1991). It suggests that the next University Funding Council review broaden the range of activities it considers when rating university research performance to include commissions by industry and commerce. This would open the way for direct recognition of the importance of these activities in considering staff for promotion and merit awards.

EFFECTIVENESS

As the preceding pages indicate, there have been a number of official programmes aimed at improving access of British industry to university-derived technology and other university-based skills and expertise. In the light of the current state of British manufacturing industry, including the high technology areas, it is difficult to conclude that these measures have been outstandingly successful. One area in which they have certainly disappointed expectations is in the transfer of technology into small companies, and the ensuing growth of a vigorous *Mittelstand* of healthy, competitive, medium-sized companies. Whether the cause lies in the operating structure of the British business environment, in the education system, in the dominance of the defence industry, or in any of the other factors which are frequently suggested, the measures taken by government have so far failed to stimulate significant expansion of this sector.

There is, however, abundant evidence that at the level of the universities there has been a very significant change in attitude. There are now extensive and rapidly growing links between UK universities and industry (frequently non-UK based), and there is evidence that these interactions are proving fruitful for all participants. Perhaps the first commercialisation of products made using genetic engineering technology, one of the main new biotechnology processes, was negotiated by Boehringer Mannheim and Noreen Murray of Edinburgh University in 1977. This led to cheaper, purer production of E. coli Pol I and T4 ligase, important enzymes used in industrial and research laboratories.

From the corporate perspective, British academics have become much more sophisticated partners in joint activities. Skill in managing joint projects varies among institutions, but the general level of understanding of industrial needs and how they can be reconciled with institutional objectives is now quite high. This means that interacting with universities has become a more straightforward and attractive option.

EXPLOITATION OF PUBLICLY FUNDED INVENTIONS

Until 1985 a government body, namely the NRDC, and then its successor the British Technology Group (BTG), had first refusal rights to any technology developed in the course of research funded by the government. It automatically retained any income generated by exploitation. Since the public purse was by far the most important source of research support at that time, there was little incentive for most universities to think about the commercial potential of the intellectual property they generated. In spite of this, the BTG had a fair measure of success in patenting and licensing. However, its spectacular failure to recognise the commercial potential of monoclonal antibody technology attracted unfavourable attention. This and the other factors discussed above led to the removal of the BTG's monopoly.

It was decided, subject to some provisos, to allow universities to retain their intellectual property rights (IPR). The BTG is destined for eventual privatisation and must now offer its brokerage services in competition with other organisations. Universities who choose to do so may dispense with its services entirely.

All universities have now formulated policies concerning IPR and exploitation, but these are still in a state of evolution. Practical experience is dictating modifications. All now wish to encourage exploitation of IPR, but there is considerable variation in the role they assign to the inventor (Bower 1992). Some strongly encourage further involvement of the inventor in developing the invention. This is a growing trend, with Cambridge at the forefront willing to disclaim its rights in IPR in favour of the inventor where the latter has a feasible strategy for exploitation. Cambridge probably has the most extensive and successful experience of academics as founders of new technology-based companies (Segal 1987). Several other universities, including Oxford and Strathclyde, are very willing to consider this course, but expect in most cases to license to an existing company or to use the BTG's services. The majority of institutions still expect to use the services of a technology broker (usually the BTG) in most cases. This is mainly because of the expense and special expertise required for direct exploitation.

As institutions acquire first- and second-hand experience, they are beginning to play a more active role. This increasing willingness for greater university and inventor participation in the innovation process was discussed in Chapters 3 and 4.

The research councils have also been given discretion over the exploitation of their in-house research, and control of any royalty revenue. They are following a similar course to the universities, but on the whole more slowly.

In most cases it has fallen to the Universities' Directors of Industrial Liaison (UDIL) or their equivalents to implement the policies, and they are playing a key role in their continuing development. They have formed a professional association which meets at regular intervals. Its working parties look at the practical realities of implementation of policies in an institutional environment. Their reports reflect these real-world concerns.

CONTROL OF INTELLECTUAL PROPERTY RIGHTS

In the UK, apart from corporate inhouse R&D which is not considered here, research which generates patentable inventions is mainly carried out in the universities, polytechnics and research council institutes.

Intellectual property rights (IPR) in patents, 'know-how', software and writing are the main potential source of income generated in these institutions. The writer's traditional ownership of copyright has been reasserted, but the other types of IPR are now controlled by the inventing institutions except where there has been a contractual disclaimer. This includes the research council institutes, whose inventions are legally the property of the Crown. The power to exploit and to dispose of any resulting income has been delegated to the individual councils themselves.

Several universities and institutes prefer to assign ownership of IPR to subsidiary companies set up for this purpose. This distances the institution from commercial transactions, which has a number of advantages. It separates functions and locates them in an appropriate vehicle. It is a tax-effective way of dealing with income from exploitation. It also makes it easier to protect the institution from any liability for inventions. Universities, particularly those with large endowments, are vulnerable to liability actions concerning products made with patented technology. Damages can be vast, especially in the American courts. Contractual disclaimers of all liability in licensing agreements, combined with legal distancing of the institution from ownership, are prudent precautions taken by many institutions in the USA and the UK.

A series of reports have made recommendations on exploitation of publicly sponsored inventions. The most recent are summarised below.

CENTRAL DIRECTION

The Scrutiny Group, whose members include representatives of all the research councils, several government offices, and the main bodies controlling higher education, issued guidelines in 1988 which recognised the importance of effective technology transfer. It recommended adoption of a flexible and pragmatic approach to exploitation of IPR. However, it pointed out that several key areas must always be addressed: identification of exploitable inventions; protection of IPR; securing exploitation; and incentivisation of inventors. It also underlined the government's preferred hierarchy of UK, EC, then non-EC companies as agents of technology transfer for inventions sponsored by public funds.

This report emphasises one point which is made repeatedly by successful practitioners of technology transfer – the importance of the inventor's continued participation in the development of the innovation. It recommends institutional encouragement and involvement.

The Department of Trade and Industry's Interdepartmental Intellectual Property Group's Report of September 1989 compared practice in UK university-based research with existing practice in the USA, Japan, West Germany and France. Apart from the UK, in most cases the institution retains at least a proportion of the IPR where there is a single sponsor. In the case of multiple sponsorship, the arrangements are varied and complex. In the UK, industrial sponsors usually own the IPR, but in the case of research council-sponsored research in the universities, the IPR remains with the host institution.

THE UDIL (1988) REPORT

The University Directors of Industrial Liaison (1988) Report urges better co-ordination, more professionalism, and proper resourcing. It complains that inventors are given excessive responsibility to recognise the potential of their inventions, and that evaluation procedures are primitive. It urges that universities should retain IPR in industrially sponsored inventions unless companies bear the full commercial costs of research. It also expresses concern that compliance with licence terms should be enforced.

UNIVERSITIES' TECHNOLOGY LICENSING PRACTICES

The universities' approaches vary; those with a long history of close interaction with industry usually have the most evolved and effective practices. Most have experienced difficulties in implementing their policies, partly from lack of enthusiasm among academics, but mainly from the much greater indifference of British companies (Bain & Co. 1990; Cohen 1990).

The first practical problem is identification of discoveries which might be exploitable. Institutions vary greatly in the extent to which they monitor research for commercial potential. Some, such as Imperial College, have or plan to institute a thorough screening procedure. This includes scanning contracts as they come in, scheduling regular meetings between members of staff and appropriate experts who can assess the commercial potential of the work, and formally requiring notification from staff if they believe their work may have commercial application. Others leave it entirely to the discretion of the member of staff and his head of department to decide whether exploitation possibilities exist. The trend is definitely towards more extensive screening. Academic staff are often ill-equipped to recognise commercial potential.

For academic research workers, there is a fundamental conflict between UK and European patent laws' restrictions on disclosure and the career requirement to publish research findings as quickly and publicly as possible. Consequently it is important that they should not only be well aware of the legal situation, including their obligations to the institution, but patenting must be made attractive by keeping the period before disclosure to the minimum (this can be a few weeks) and by offering a significant share of the financial rewards. This problem has been addressed by the more far-sighted institutions, which undertake to complete their preliminary assessment of inventions and application formalities within a few weeks. However, not all institutions appreciate the scientist's point of view. Consequently they do not all give speed of assessment sufficient priority.

The question of incentives is also receiving careful consideration. Where the total sums are small, some institutions give all or most of the royalties (net of costs) to the inventor, taking a larger proportion as the amounts grow. This is a good 'marketing' move, to spread interest among academic staff.

When preliminary assessment indicates commercial potential, the DIL moves on to the next stage. In the case of publicly funded research, three possible avenues are considered:

1 The institution may invite the BTG or the other major technology broker operating in the UK, 3I Research Exploitation Ltd, to commercialise an invention. The broker will assess its potential uses and its market. If they fit with its (demanding) commercial criteria, the broker will undertake to patent, protect and attempt to license the invention. The usual arrangement is that the broker takes ownership and in exchange returns 50 per cent of net royalty income to the institution.

2 The institution (or its subsidiary technology licensing company) may patent the invention and directly seek a licensee.

3 The institution may patent the invention or assign IPR to the inventor(s) and then assist in direct exploitation, often via a campus-based start-up involving the inventor(s). Finance from a university/private syndicate is sometimes available.

With industrially funded research, the contract will usually specify the procedure for notifying the sponsor, the rights of the institution, and the claims to IPR or licensing option of the sponsor. There is a move on the universities' part towards retaining greater rights in IPR, especially when the research has not been fully funded at commercial rates.

Where the industrial sponsor wishes collaboration to develop the invention, the inventor is often willing to enter into a further contractual arrangement on the same basis as before for this purpose. Alternatively, some institutions now offer purpose-built incubator facilities for commercial development or the possibility of a joint venture on a campus science park. The precise route chosen depends on acceptability and availability.

Some institutions, notably UMIST, are offering services which when taken together amount to complete collaborative development, taking the invention from the laboratory, through the prototype stage to production planning, instrumentation and control.

RESEARCH COUNCIL INSTITUTES

The role of the research council institutes

Commercial activities in the research units and institutes operated directly by the government's research councils are regulated by the differing policies of their respective councils. They have also been urged by the government to take an active role in promoting commercial exploitation of their expertise and inventions.

Many of the institutes have a long history of interaction with industry and agribusiness. In some cases their original role was specifically to provide advisory services and research back-up to the commercial sector. Since these services were, until recently, mostly free of charge or at a nominal rate, a commercial attitude had never developed in the organisations themselves.

IPR

While the rights to IPR generated in the universities by contract research have been assigned to the inventing institutions as described above, ownership of IPR generated in the research councils' own institutes lies formally with the Crown. The effective control over IPR and licensing royalties has been devolved to the councils themselves, and their position is functionally similar to that of the universities. Exploitation is governed by policies set up independently by each council.

They have been slower than the universities to consider the desirability of encouraging invention by significantly rewarding inventors. This is changing and official policies are all under review. The guidelines at present are as follows:

AFRC

The Agriculture and Food Research Council has a large number of institutes carrying out research over a very broad range, from basic animal, viral and plant molecular biology to the most applied topics.

The AFRC's practice in dealing with IPR and exploitation of inventions depends on the sources of funds for a given project. Where work is sponsored by the Ministry of Agriculture, IPR remains with the ministry. This is usually also the case with industrial sponsors if they have paid full cost, although there is then a revenue-sharing arrangement.

Where work is funded out of the AFRC's own resources, the policy is to leave IPR and responsibility for exploitation with the institutes themselves. These have used different procedures. Where companies have sponsored research, IPR is sometimes assigned to the company, but has also on occasion been retained by the institute concerned. Where rights are retained, institutes have either obtained legal advice about patenting and licensing from Head Office, or have dealt directly with professional advisers. They have sometimes chosen to use the services of the BTG or other agencies, and sometimes acted entirely on their own account.

There is no automatic right of the inventors to any share of the rewards, although the AFRC participates in the Ministry of Defence COATI scheme which gives awards only in outstanding cases. The MRC used also to belong to this scheme but has rejected it in favour of more generous arrangements. At present the AFRC is also thinking of developing an in-house scheme, geared to its own needs. The new guidelines should be available before the end of 1990.

MRC

The Medical Research Council currently spends approximately £100m per annum on research within its own units and institutes (MRC Annual Report, 1988-9). It carries out basic and applied research on topics of relevance to medicine. The council has a very heavy commitment to molecular genetics, a field in which it has sponsored some of the most significant discoveries of the last 30 years. It boasts a large number of Nobel prize-winners among the staff of its units.

The MRC has moved farther and faster than the other research councils towards creating structures for effective exploitation of its research. It has set up an Industrial Liaison Group at head office, and has also opened a Collaborative Centre. Its policy is also currently under revision. The general form of the revised policy is as follows, although note that it has not been finalised yet.

The onus lies with members of staff who consider that their work may have commercial potential, to notify their Director, who is then expected to take appropriate action. He/she will normally inform the Industrial Liaison Group at head office.

After notification, there are several courses open. The MRC may use the services of the BTG or 3I's REL (see Chapter 5). Alternatively, the MRC Collaborative Centre may offer assistance with patenting, licensing and also facilities for joint development with industrial sponsors. There are also limited possibilities of developing or licensing through Celltech Ltd, an independent private company. Whatever the chosen course, the MRC prefers to leave obtaining and defending patents to outside organisations, although it may be willing to submit the initial application.

Except where income is generated from collaborative agreements (when it is normally credited to the unit), net royalties are payable to inventors and their units, with a relatively large proportion going to the inventor when total sums are small.

SERC

The Science and Engineering Research Council supports several major central research facilities for the use of the scientific community. In 1988, about £96m was allocated to them. They include radiotelescopes, synchrotron and neutron radiation sources. An Industrial Liaison Unit has been set up at the Synchrotron to develop industrial applications. Currently, studies on superconductors are in progress at the neutron source. It also runs a number of joint university/industry research programmes, designed to plug technology gaps. These 'clubs' are also expected to accustom members to interdisciplinary and inter-organisational collaboration.

The SERC recognises the value of the flexible and pragmatic approach recommended by the Scrutiny Group. Its policy is currently under review and is expected to follow the same general direction as the universities.

NERC

The National Environment Research Council has research institutes carrying out research on a wide range of topics including marine biology, earth sciences, climate and atmospheric sciences. Its extensive facilities include marine research vessels and stations in the Antarctic.

NERC set up a Corporate Affairs Unit in 1989. It offers funds for collaborative projects with industry. Extractive industry geology is one current focus of support.

The NERC's policy on IPR and exploitation is under review. It will probably follow the same path as the other organisations. Inventors are entitled to claim compensation, but no guidelines indicating the probable amounts have been published yet.

INFORMATION SOURCES FOR INDUSTRIAL LIAISON

The importance of transferring technology is now widely recognised in British publicly funded institutions with a significant involvement in research. Most have developed policies on exploitation and to a variable degree they have created the structures and facilities to implement them. However in many organisations the information flows, which are essential for making these policies effective, are imperfect.

Effective and regular circulation of information between staff and industrial liaison offices is crucially important for the operation of the structures that have been set up to assist technology transfer. Equally essential is that information about expertise, services and licensing opportunities should be conveyed to potential clients. Some institutions have excellent arrangements for informing researchers of their rights and responsibilities, and also of keeping them up to date with the institution's own mechanisms for assisting in implementation. Unfortunately, this is the exception. A 1989 MORI poll carried out for the BTG revealed a lack of guidance for the staff in many UK institutions. Most need to increase their efforts to keep the various parties to the transfer enterprise fully informed and interested in what is going on.

With such a large number of medium-sized organisations each with many areas of specialisation, there are obvious problems in matching institutional skills, services and inventions with potential clients. This is a matter which needs a great deal of thought and planning. The information available is increasing, but it is still difficult to locate.

Currently available

Offices of industrial liaison are publishing a growing number of leaflets to keep industry informed of their current areas of expertise, services on offer, etc. These vary in their usefulness.

Several, including Cambridge, Edinburgh and Strathclyde Universities, publish a regular newsletter for industry, highlighting current work of industrial interest. Strathclyde's quarterly newsletter is particularly well presented and even includes a list of patents available for licensing. Most publications are less specific in their coverage, only listing areas of expertise and services.

There are also commercial publications and databases covering UK institutions' skills, services and licensing opportunities (see Appendix). They are inevitably incomplete in their coverage but they are inexpensive and accessible. Some international databases give good coverage of the UK and Europe, e.g. CAB International's Abstracts which gives excellent coverage of agriculture/ biotechnology (see Appendix).

The traditional information sources, are, of course, still in use. Scanning the scientific literature, nowadays with the assistance of computerised search facilities, and personal contact at conferences or through visits to laboratories, are still highly effective ways of locating expertise or new ideas.

EFFECTIVE TRANSFER

According to the MORI (1989) report, while about half of the UK heads of departments and researchers polled had seriously thought of setting up their own company, very few would think of asking their institution to assist them in developing inventions. Once again, the information flows have been deficient. There is now an increasing possibility of institutional support, in several shapes and forms.

Most institutions with a significant research capacity are creating some capacity for inhouse development, whether in a special facility or in a campus company. The evidence from all sides strongly suggests that this approach greatly enhances the success of technology transfer at the most difficult stage in the innovative process.

The enthusiasm to develop the project is present in many of the inventing scientists, and the means for further development and for joint ventures with industry are being put in place by the universities. This should lead to a steady increase in the number of projects being carried to the point at which commercial potential can be assessed much more accurately by external groups. This reduction in uncertainty ought, in turn, to lead to fewer business ideas being abandoned. Once again, the effectiveness of the mechanisms being put in place will depend in part on all the interested parties being aware of their availability.

A point which has been repeatedly made by the Scrutiny Group and by UDIL in both the USA and the UK concerns the problem of bridging the transition from the original invention to the point at which the developing innovation is fully integrated into the industrial R&D process. They emphasise that this transition requires a high level of commitment both from the inventor and from the sponsoring company. There is usually a need for further work to be carried out by the inventor in a closer relationship with the company. This is necessary to take the technology to a point at which the company's structure can cope with it. Success in the transfer process requires a great deal of effort and good will on both sides of the inventor/company joint venture, if the invention is not to wither on the branch.

A 'champion' in the company hierarchy is also seen to be important: an individual who has a commitment to the invention and who has sufficiently high standing within the company to smooth the transfer of the technology to the company. This parallels the role of 'champion' in companies' own in-house research, which is often found to be of key importance in studies of successful product development.

The message that comes from all sides is that successful technology transfer requires an enthusiastic commitment from the inventor, an actively supportive institutional environment, and keen involvement of an executive with significant actualisation power within the sponsoring company. The will is there to meet all these conditions within the new structures being created on UK campuses.

THE RESPONSE OF INDUSTRY

The climate for transfer is becoming favourable within the universities and research institutes in Britain. Companies are generally availing themselves of the opportunities (see Chapter 9). However, the message from the UK's own industry is not so positive. Only one-fifth of Oxford University's rapidly increasing industrial sponsorship comes from British companies (Clark 1985). UK universities as a group receive one-third of their industrial sponsorship from non-UK companies (Fishlock 1990). The UK is a net exporter of new, university-generated ideas (BTG 1989, 1990). Even the British pharmaceutical business is less interested in joint ventures on campus or with small companies than are its European, Japanese and American rivals; and this is a sector in which the UK still has a significant, world-class industry. In other sectors, too, American or Japanese companies are more likely to snap up the new ideas and inventions (Mackenzie and Jones 1985).

This obviously makes the task of the British Directors of Industrial Liaison more difficult and expensive than it would be if there were large numbers of interested local companies to deal with. Whether or not relationships with foreign companies are acceptable, these foreign companies are not likely to be interested in many of the individually less important inventions which, cumulatively, may be of very great importance. Thus much of the investment may be lost.

The mountain is coming to Muhammad

However, growing numbers of international companies are demonstrably willing to engage in collaboration over long distances with British scientists. In addition, it is no longer unusual for companies to site R&D facilities near universities in other countries, to be near the source of invention. Many international companies including Switzerland's Ciba-Geigy and Japan's Yamanouchi now have R&D laboratories in the UK.

The rate of growth of innovative activity which characterises the current lively scene in the UK parallels that in the USA. The very practical approach of the institutions has allowed them to respond quite flexibly to the varied requirements of the innovative process.

Chapter 5

Science parks and technology transfer

Most of the government-inspired initiatives to encourage technological innovation in the USA and the UK have drawn at least some of their inspiration from the visible success of the many small, high technology companies clustered around Stanford University and MIT in the USA, which draw continuing support from the campus. Their potential to act as a channel for the diffusion of new technology into industry has attracted a great deal of interest. The encouragement of the science park phenomenon has thus played an important role in most countries' efforts to stimulate technology transfer from universities.

There is some debate as to whether these parks have indeed contributed significantly to economic development. Certainly, few have had the success of the pioneers. However, they have many supporters and they are now such an integral part of the technology transfer scene that some knowledge of their history and current extent is a prerequisite for interpreting governments' policies for industrial innovation.

THE ROLE OF THE SCIENCE PARK

The science park movement has grown out of the perception that the process of developing innovative technologies and products has special requirements for inputs which are often not available within an individual company's own establishment. The other belief that has fuelled the recent rapid expansion of the movement is that innovative technology is the key to economic success. The various interest groups who are concerned with economic development and innovation have come together in many locations around the world to try to create environments in which innovation can be fostered.

In recent years, governmental bodies, universities, companies and financiers have attempted to find the ideal formula for university/industry interaction.

The science park is a communal venture, bringing together several complementary groups to nurture the growth of technology-based enterprises. Several interest groups normally participate. They include research-oriented universities; development organisations associated with the universities; small, technology-based companies; R&D laboratories of large companies, and communal service centres. They also include the financial backers of the tenants of the park, the interested higher education institutions and corporate sponsors. Local government is frequently involved as a founder, a backer of companies, and as a general sponsor.

THE EARLY PARKS

The idea of the science park has grown out of the collaborations between industry and universities, which resulted, in a few celebrated early cases, in a considerable growth in the high technology business sector in the vicinity of the university. Spin-out companies from the university, large company R&D establishments, and university/industry collaborative development organisations are all typical tenants of the park, which is either on campus, or at least very nearby.

The most famous examples include the successful symbiosis between Stanford, its science park and Silicon Valley (Saxenian 1983); MIT and the cluster of high technology companies on Route 128 in Boston (Roberts 1968); and the Cambridge Science Park phenomenon in England (Segal 1987). In all these cases, continuing close interaction between a major research university and a group of high technology spin-out companies has led to successful technology transfer and a considerable boost to the local economy.

These initial ventures developed in a more *laissez-faire* atmosphere, although in a very supportive setting, with the conscious involvement of highly motivated individuals in the universities and other participating organisations. Now the parties which have a local interest in innovation and high technology business get together to design science parks down to the last detail. It has become a highly fashionable way to address a group of problems: the revitalisation of declining regional economies; the need to maximise the perceived return to the tax-paying community from universities' basic research; the nurture of small hitech businesses; and, finally, generally to foster technological innovation. The belief is that all these matters can be addressed to greater effect by a unified approach.

FACTORS FOR SUCCESS

Several factors have been important for the success of the longer-established parks. The first is the presence of a major technological university (Giersch 1985). It plays the core roles of providing expertise, manpower, facilities, spin-offs, and attracting large companies' R&D divisions. While some so-called 'science parks' have been set up which lacked a university focus, they are not considered here.

The second major factor is the firm commitment from influential individuals in the university, the surrounding community and its business institutions to the success of the park. The other significant variables are less precisely defined as: an attractive living and working environment; a good structure for interactions between companies, university and community; availability of financial resources; and similar relational aspects.

The entrepreneurial community itself becomes a determining factor in the equation – the cultural support of belonging to a work community sharing the same values and addressing the same problems.

EXTRAORDINARY FACTORS

It has been suggested several times that the Silicon Valley and Route 128 stories only achieved success because of extraordinary factors. The most obvious of these is that both were focused on universities that already had large, outstanding and famous research establishments in science and engineering, with an attractive power to industry that most institutions must inevitably lack. The other point which has sometimes been made is that probably neither of them would have created viable businesses without the availability of massive support from Department of Defense contracts.

These comments may have some validity, at least in that the ultimate scale of the economic growth engendered around these parks may be unlikely to occur very often. The contribution of defence funding cannot, however, be cited as a factor in the biotechnology revolution. The energy of American entrepreneurs in finding ways of turning circumstances to their own advantage must be acknowledged. The science park formula has stood the test of application in less promising circumstances, and still produced very good results, if less spectacular than these early models.

Take, for instance, the development of the Heriot-Watt Research Park, the first to be founded in Europe, in 1969. Plans were drawn up following the visit of two senior professors at Heriot-Watt to Stanford and MIT and their environments, including the constellation of companies which had sprung up around them (Childs and Smart 1966). Careful attention was paid to the mutually sustaining relationships between the universities, the companies, and other vocational training establishments in the area that supplied technical staff to the companies. Heriot-Watt's core activity had always been the provision of services to local industry, including training and research, and the visitors examined closely all these aspects of the interrelationships between industry and educational institutions.

Manpower problems have not been looked at very closely in most studies of these science parks. The assumption has been that the major universities provided the skills. This was true only for a proportion of founders and employees. The Heriot-Watt team were impressed by the close attention to industrial needs for skilled technicians paid by San José State and Foothill College, in California, and by North Eastern in Boston. The latter university, which at that time offered only part-time sandwich courses, trained working technicians to BS level in 5 years and to MS in 6. There was no suggestion that quality suffered from the division of students' time between work and study – there were no vacations.

The visit to Stanford was arranged by Hewlett-Packard, the Stanford spin-out company, whose subsidiary a few miles from Heriot-Watt had close links with the university. The Boston visit was arranged by Arthur D. Little Inc., whose nineteenth-century founder was himself an MIT graduate. The plan was implemented by Heriot-Watt's Principal (1967–74), Robert Smith, a Scotsman who had previously been a Professor at MIT and Director of MIT's Center for Material Science and Engineering. It is probable that his appointment was in itself an immediate consequence of Smart and Childs' visit.

Thus the circle was closed, and the European technical high school modelled its next phase on the model of the successful Americans who had looked to Europe in the nineteenth century for the institutional structures from which their indigenous style had evolved. The Heriot-Watt Research Park was accordingly set up with close attention to the principles of these American models, but with full awareness of the local situation. The injunction of the then Chairman of Arthur D. Little Inc., Raymond Stevens, not to divorce the university from the community was unnecessary for an institution already fully committed to that principle.

The situation of Heriot-Watt at that time was not particularly auspicious, in an area suffering from decline of its traditional industries. The university itself had only about 1,000 students in 1970, and was desperately underfunded throughout the 1970s. As far as government support was concerned, it remained so for several more years and is still sparingly supported from the centre. Its funding has had to come increasingly from private and corporate sources.

This has not inhibited its steady development and the healthy growth of the research park. Today there are thirty-five organisations on the park, of which most have roots in the university, either as development organisations or as spin-outs. The longer-established development organisations are now self-funding, and have themselves spun out companies. Three US companies have R&D subsidiaries on the park. In 1989 the park was full, with demand still rising, and the university purchased a further 100 acres to extend its area.

The development organisations all follow the same pattern. They are interdisciplinary, closely integrated with the university, bringing together research teams to work on industrial problems and offering specialised consultancy and other services to their associated companies, often through consultancy subsidiaries. The development organisations and the companies on the park cover several industries, and are entirely international, but the connecting rationale is usually local: for example, the Institute of Offshore Engineering has always had close links with the North Sea oil industry, but through its expertise in oil-related water pollution has developed towards the growing environmental business. This expertise has attracted companies like Millipore and the Forth River Purification Board to set up on the park.

The longstanding links with the brewing and distilling industries, international but again with a strong local focus, has led to formal establishment of a development organisation in 1990 – the International Centre for Brewing and Distilling – with funds from the UK industry associations and from Japan's Suntory. This area of expertise has also diversified and now there are also growing involvements with the food processing, aquaculture and environmental industries, again with multidisciplinary links within the university, and a group of medium and large companies on the outside.

The Computer Advisory Service, established in the very early days to assist local industry to integrate computer technology into manufacturing processes, has followed the lines of computer technology as it has evolved towards a range of expertise with emphasis on novel telecoms applications.

At the same time the university has grown in student (now 5,000) and staff numbers and in the range and depth of research. In 1989 it drew about 27 per cent of its funds from research contracts and provision of services, and of this three-quarters came from industrial sources. Clearly the park and the university have enjoyed symbiotic growth. But what about the benefits to the wider community? Beyond the jobs and turnover created within the park, have there been other economic benefits?

This is less easy to assess, but the signs are positive. The City of Edinburgh, along with developers who will provide the cash, has planned another, larger technology park a mile or so from the university. The success of the development organisations on the Park has led to the award, jointly with Edinburgh University, of funds for a Petroleum Engineering Centre, to be sited on the Park. The money will come from a consortium including the Department of Trade and Industry and oil companies.

More generally, in spite of the worldwide recession in 1990, at that date the Scottish economy looked healthier than at any time since the First World War. In 1991, with the UK still in the depths of recession, Scotland for the first time was hit less severely than the south east of England: Heriot-Watt and its science park can reasonably claim some share of the credit.

The precise relationship between all these favourable outcomes and the determination of the Heriot-Watt Research Park founders to follow the principles of Stanford and MIT in industrial liaison and science park development will never be determined. But there is no doubt that considerable successes have been achieved, in circumstances less obviously favourable than those which attended the growth of Silicon Valley and Route 128.

THE GROWTH PATTERN OF A PARK

The growth of parks is characterised by two phases (Giersch 1985). The first is the period during which the founders, usually the university in collaboration with local government and local financial institutions, sets up the initial ground-plan, to include the initial research facilities, incubators and offices, services, and sometimes housing. The layout and landscaping are an important part of the general attractiveness of the location. The less visible parts of the infrastructure are equally important for maintaining the growth potential of the park. This period typically takes several years, during which there is little employment growth.

The next phase, which also serves as an indicator for the future success of the park, is the period during which new companies start to set up in the park. Often these are direct or indirect spin-offs from the university. This is the period which generates new, highly skilled jobs and the beginning of the economic returns in the shape of a lively, innovative local corporate sector.

APPLYING THE FORMULA

Science parks are springing up throughout Europe, the USA and the Far East. Several are briefly described here to illustrate the kinds of formulas that are being employed. Some have been operating for quite a long time, but the vast majority were founded after 1980.

USA

The Research Triangle Park of North Carolina was founded in the late 1950s to encourage high technology industry to locate in North Carolina. The founders were a group of influential financiers, industrialists and politicians. Private and state funds underpinned its initial stages. The park is managed by a foundation which returns profits from the Park to supporting joint research and educational projects involving the three universities which are linked to the park.

The early tenants were major companies such as Monsanto and

IBM. By 1986, 20,000 people worked in thirty-five organisations on the Park (Waugaman 1986). However, the first organisation set up was a non-profit research institute which carried out collaborative projects between university scientists and private or public sponsors. There has been more emphasis on small business development in recent years.

In 1980 the Microelectronics Center of North Carolina was established by Governor Hunt. It received $82m of state funding in its first 6 years of operation. Its purpose was to train many more students in modern electronics and to provide first-rate research and training facilities. It co-ordinates activities at five universities and has a laboratory on the Park. They are linked with the centre and with one another by a complex network of videoconferencing facilities and by a Very Large-Scale Integrated (VLSI) circuit design computer sytem with terminals at all sites.

The Microelectronics Center had seven affiliate companies supporting its programme in 1986, and a total of 15–20 are eventually expected to join. They pay annual fees and help plan and direct a research project funded by their subscriptions. They receive other benefits, including collaborative research opportunities for their staff. Several major companies have located facilities in the vicinity in the expectation that the centre will be useful to them.

A Biotechnology Center was set up in 1981, with similar aims and range of support, but somewhat less state funding. It has attracted support from the NSF, the Naval Research Office and the Department of Agriculture for multi-institutional programmes. The Biotechnology Center has an office in the park, but no central laboratory. The universities' facilities are reckoned to be adequate.

Growth in population and in the number of jobs in the area has been considerable. Low taxes, a pleasant environment, a good infrastructure and cheap land have been factors in the success of the park. North Carolina was the first state to use this strategy to attract companies, and this was probably a reason for its success.

In North Carolina, a large number of programmes to promote technological innovation have been set up over the last 30 years. They were initiated by a series of state Governors who were all concerned to encourage economic development but also to reflect the diversity of interests of their founders. They are not part of an overall plan and are funded through and audited by a variety of agencies. Ultimately they are all dependent on the state's General

Assembly for funding. This means that so long as the political climate favours state support of industrial innovation, a wide array of groups and organisations are sponsored to pursue this general objective through the universities, other educational services, industrial research centres, small business services and other state bodies (Waugaman 1986). This diversity obviously poses problems for effective management by the state's leadership.

Sweden

Sweden's Novum Research Park, officially opened in 1990, is expected to house both Swedish and foreign companies and organisations developing healthcare products. It has close links with the Karolinska Institute and its medical school, which has a research institute on the park. It is planned to build a new, research-oriented international university in the park itself, around a nucleus of Professors already in the Karolinska Institute Medical and Odontology Schools.

At present (1990), one start-up company, five large-company R&D subsidiaries (including Kabi and Procordia), three development organisations and two medical school departments are located on the park. There is also a government organisation, SPRIMA, which tests medical products and assists the health services in their procurement policies.

Germany

Medical Park Hanover, projected to become Europe's premier bioscience centre, was opened in 1987. Germany is Europe's biggest market for pharmaceutical and medical electronics companies. Biotechnica Hannover has established itself as the major European annual trade fair in this sector. Thus from the market perspective, the location is excellent. Hanover also hosts more than 100 educational centres, with the medical school next door to the park.

Not surprisingly, several large German companies have set up facilities there, as has Invitron Inc., a US biotechnology company. The Max Planck Institute for Experimental Endocrinology and the Fraunhofer Institute for Toxicology and Aerosol Research are also situated in the park. Absent, at present, are the spin-outs from the university which are a standard feature of US and UK parks.

France

Sophia Antipolis, in the French Alpes Maritimes, is a science park on a grand scale, almost a technological utopia. Set up in 1969 by a core of engineers and scientists from the Ecole des Mines in Paris, together with the regional government and local innovators, its initial development phase took 15 years. Surprisingly, in a country with little provincial science and technological activity, it has moved steadily towards success. It is now well into the second phase, with new companies setting up and effective technology transfer occurring (Laffitte 1985). It now houses many companies, including multinationals, research organisations and laboratories of the University of Nice, l'Ecole des Mines and Ceram. In 1985 it employed 5,000 workers and covered about 7,000 acres. It is planning a considerable expansion in the near future.

Japan

Similar initiatives are being taken in Japan (Laffitte 1985), where start-ups are rare, but science/technology joint ventures are now strongly encouraged in 'science cities'. The first of these, Tsukuba science city, is fairly well established now. It was set up by moving a university out of Tokyo to a country site, surrounding it with major government research institutes, and inviting large companies to set up R&D centres on the periphery. The whole plan was put together by the government, and companies have duly set up labs around the city, joined increasingly by foreign companies. Its effectiveness is impossible to assess at present, but the model has aroused great enthusiasm within Japan. Another is planned by the region that contains the prestigious Kyoto University. This institution, lacking space to expand in Kyoto, will be moved into the hills of Kansai prefecture and surrounded by public and private sector laboratories along the lines of the Tsukuba venture.

DEVELOPMENT ORGANISATIONS

The main bridging structure between the university laboratory and the large company laboratory is the 'development organisation'. The term includes a range of organisations which all have the general features of being set up by a consortium, including nowadays at least one university and several sources of financial and industrial support. These may include technology broking organisations or venture capitalists, who include some special expertise in transferring technology in the package of support they bring to the enterprise.

Their aim is to bring together university and company scientists in an environment in which both sides can function happily. Activities are focused around specific R&D projects, but the hope is that the nature of the environment will stimulate a deeper understanding by the parties of one another's needs. This, in turn, is expected to lead to more effective work on current projects and also to a more productive formulation of ideas in other areas in which a joint approach could be useful.

Attempts have long been made to set up such organisations on campus, since MIT's 1916 Laboratory of Chemistry. Results have been mixed: some have become permanent, self-funding entities, such as SRI International, now completely independent of its parent, Stanford; others have faltered and declined. Among these are the attempts in the early 1960s to develop university/industry interactions in Michigan (Baba and Hart 1986). Remarkably little evaluation work has been done on the more established of these ventures. In spite of this, there is a general conviction that they are valuable, and considerable sums are being spent currently to create many more of them.

While it is difficult to analyse and compare these very diverse organisations in the search for patterns associated with success, some factors do appear to be important. They are very directly related to the depth of knowledge of the other's world that characterises the future partners at the founding of the organisation. They may be summarised as follows.

1 The organisation must in some way enhance the academics' basic research capability. Only thus can it offer a reward to them for their involvement. This is so central to the career success of academic scientists that their interest will not persist in its absence. The experience of the Michigan CIM centre (Baba and Hart 1986) has been that academic interest has faded rapidly in a highly goal-directed institute.

2 The setting-up stage is of crucial importance, not only for setting the ground rules but also for imbuing the enterprise with sufficient prestige to win a commitment from the desired partners. Gray *et al.* (1986a) remark of the NSF Centers Program

that the involvement of NSF was important for several reasons, not least because their peer review of projects validated the quality and assisted the marketing of the whole enterprise. NSF's involvement at the initial stage was also useful because of their unusual depth of experience of the institutions and individuals on the science side, and their accumulation of experience in actually putting together such centres.

3 Formal communications systems – when these organisations are set up there is usually great emphasis on facilitating *informal* communication, indeed this is often a major objective. What is less well planned is the formal system, which ensures continuing involvement by all parties, particularly at times when the informal system may be less effective. This was another feature regarded as important for success in the NSF centres (Gray *et al.* 1986a).

NETWORKING BEYOND THE PARK

An interesting development of the science park concept is the European Business and Innovation Centre Network (EBN), set up by the EEC in 1984. This recognises the needs of small new companies for training and other support services, including specialised information. Parks that join the scheme are assisted to set up a Business Information Centre (BIC) which will provide some of these services directly, but which will also have access through an electronic network to information held by other BICs. This allows the BIC to act as a matching point for joint venture partners, as an agent for the procurement of technologies, and in other ways which are helpful to the companies on the linked parks throughout the EC.

In the USA, the organisation NAMTAC is filling a similar role, linking organisations concerned with business development and technology transfer in a quasi trade/professional association.

ASSESSING THE TRACK RECORD

There are records of failure. During the recession of 1958–61 a whole series of science and technology collaboration initiatives was planned by the State of Michigan. During the economic upturn in the mid-1960s, they attracted little interest and did not achieve anything of significance. A contributory cause may have been that they lacked focus and firm financial support (Baba and Hart 1986).

Another Michigan experiment, which is developing rather differently from the original plan, is the Industrial Technology Institute, opened in 1981 with an ambitious programme focused on development of computer-integrated manufacturing. It was set up as an independent organisation, although with statutory links to all the research universities in the state. It received $67m in private and public funding from industry, the state, organised labour and foundations to finance its early stages.

Its mission was to concentrate resources on CIM, reckoned to be the key technological area for the state's future industrial health. It was not placed physically on any of the campuses, in order to avoid any dilution of its own mission. The state's research universities had no particular strength in this field, but it was believed that a first-rate, well-financed R&D centre would attract the necessary talent.

The initial programme of research was very market oriented. Four years after its foundation, relationships with industrial sponsors were growing, but the early connections with universities had mostly weakened or been lost (Baba and Hart 1986). The pressures which have resulted in this state of affairs include political and industrial pressure for speedy applications. It is an outstanding example of a goal-directed project in which 'best science' objectives have no place.

It is not surprising that university interest has not been sustained, since objectives which would enhance the career opportunities for academics have been excluded from the institute's charter. The initial desire to involve university and industrial scientists appears to have lost sight of the need to offer appropriate incentives to both sides.

The Higuchi Biosciences Center at the University of Kansas (Charles Decedue, personal communication) has avoided these pitfalls by continually striving to match the needs of all the participants. Its success has led to the decision to set up three additional development organisations on the campus by 1992 (KTEC 1989).

Probably the single most important factor for success in these enterprises is the personal qualities of the key individuals. It is remarked by many writers that the involvement of highly motivated, talented people within the component organisations, who form networks to pursue the aims of the various joint ventures and the science park as a whole, are crucial to the survival and positive achievement of the enterprise (Gray *et al.* 1986b; Segal Quince Wicksteed 1988; Nelsen 1988a). These are the 'champions' of the technology transfer project within their own organisation, who build the bridges with the partner organisations.

Other factors

The emphasis here has been on the institutional factors and the relationships between companies and universities which affect outcomes. Very little has been said concerning the general environmental factors that have played a role in the rapid growth of parks. The physical attractiveness of the surroundings, the availability of good housing and schools, and the support of a welcoming community are critically important in drawing and keeping the highly skilled workforce which powers the science park's development. Their significance should not be underestimated in the planning of parks.

Criteria for assessing success

Here is a possible checklist for measuring the success of a science park, using the measures that have most commonly been employed thus far:

1 Willingness of developers to fund construction, in spite of being constrained by the requirements set for companies locating in the park.
2 Ability to attract private sector investment.
3 Continuing relationships between the university and the park tenants.
4 Number of spin-outs, joint ventures, etc.
5 Failure rates.
6 Reasons for moving.
7 Expansion of young firms.
8 Local development stimulated by the park.
9 Increase in university and its staff's incomes attributable to the park.
10 Enhancement of the reputation of the participants by association.

CONCLUSION

Both in their history and in their current manifestations, science parks have been a rather diverse phenomenon. Their absolute success has also been variable. Part of this is no doubt owing to the fact that many have been set up in areas that were already suffering severe economic disadvantages which could not be overcome by limited local efforts to swim against the tide.

At present, the jury is still out on science parks, but they continue to attract enthusiastic supporters throughout the industrialised world. In time there will undoubtedly be a sufficient body of data with which to measure their contribution to economic progress.

Chapter 6

University/industry liaison in other countries

Considerable attention is being given to liaison between universities, government-funded research institutes, and companies throughout the industrialised world. However, it is beyond the scope of this book to look in detail at the global picture. Some small countries such as Sweden and Switzerland have been outstanding performers in this area for a long time, but they must be omitted from this discussion. A brief overview of the main industrial countries is essential, however, to provide a context for analysis of the American and British scenes.

JAPAN

Japanese institutions, both public and private, devote an enormous amount of attention to forecasting the direction of technical and social change (Freeman 1987; Yamauchi 1986). Future needs are identified, and great efforts are made to ensure that science and technology develop in ways that will serve them.

Japanese officials and industrialists have been concerned for some time to foster invention in Japan. The technologies on which they have built their economic success were initially imported from the west. The Japanese have to a great extent accepted the western view of themselves, that although enormously innovative, they are not inventive. Some have stated that the Japanese are culturally incapable of invention. This is highly questionable, but it does appear that their scientific institutions have hitherto discouraged invention. Influential Japanese such as Tonegawa, the expatriate Nobel laureate who claimed his work would have been impossible within the framework of a Japanese institution, have blamed organisational structures for the perceived lack of creativity.

On the other hand, the Japanese are exceptionally punctilious about correctly attributing origins. They still refer to the many deities which they originally adopted from elsewhere as foreign. These were mostly integrated into Japanese culture during the same era in which Christianity was adopted by Western Europe. There were no apologies in the latter case for lack of creativity.

Most observers of the Japanese scene report that Japan is catching up with the west in scientific achievements in many areas. References to Japanese scientists in the *Journal of Applied Physics* grew from 2–3 per cent in 1964 to 23 per cent in 1982 (Phillips 1989). Along with this is coming an increasing level of invention, although there are still arguments about how much of this is incremental rather than major saltatory invention (Fransman 1990; Moritani 1991). This notion that Japanese invention may possibly be less radical than that of the west may console Westerners who are slipping behind in the economic competition. Japan is nevertheless an increasing source of new technology for the rest of the world – in 1990 the US spent $491m to license Japanese technology (Moffat 1991).

Japanese academic industrial liaison

Japanese academic/industrial liaison until recently came in only two forms: one in which both parties were Japanese, the other in which the corporate partner was Japanese and the academic partner non-Japanese. This is beginning to change (Moffat 1991), but there are still few instances of western companies liaising with Japanese scientists. Where they occur, the companies are Japan-based subsidiaries of foreign companies. This may be more a function of western reluctance to learn to read Japanese and to locate in Japan than of Japanese desire to exclude foreign interests (ibid.). On the whole, foreigners visiting or working in Japan report a very communicative atmosphere, and great availability of information about scientific and technological developments (Fransman 1990; Moffat 1991; Bower 1991a).

Accounts of individual collaboration are rare. A recent letter to *Nature* (Scheidegger 1990) related very positive experiences by a scientist working in Ciba-Geigy's International Research Laboratories in Japan. This laboratory is engaged in joint projects with several Japanese university laboratories.

At present, industrial liaison between Japanese academic

scientists and non-Japanese companies outside Japan is probably impossible. Japanese universities are forbidden by the Ministry of Education to accept foreign funds. Recently, when Japanese scientists were awarded grants under the Japanese Human Frontiers Science Programme which is based in Strasburg, they had to accept the money personally and 'gift' it to their universities. They were then taxed on the original sum as though it had been income. Not surprisingly this caused an outcry, which was eventually resolved not by lifting the ban, but by the Ministry of Finance giving Human Frontiers grants a special status (*Nature* 1990a).

In the meantime, then, while it is of interest to look at the mechanisms of industrial/academic interchange in Japan and their successes, direct involvement is unlikely to be particularly attractive to outsiders who have no Japanese base.

Industrial liaison within research-oriented institutions in Japan

In Japan there are several types of academic institution involved in potentially exploitable research. The most important of these are the universities, which fall into three categories, and the national research institutes. Initially the research institutes had the main responsibility for interacting with industry. However, Japanese government policy has moved towards encouraging such activity for university staff as well.

The universities

The universities are under pressure to do more basic research, and simultaneously to transfer more technology to industry. Only three have much experience of this. In 1985, Sendai, Osaka and Tokyo Institute of Technology had generated more than half of all university patents (Clark 1985).

The national (formerly imperial) universities are the highest status group among the universities. Their funding comes mainly from Monbusho, the government's Ministry of Education. The regional governments or prefectures maintain another group of universities. Then there are the private universities, by far the largest category, but focused with a few exceptions on the less expensive, non-science-based disciplines.

In 1983, universities spent Y904bn of public money and Y745bn of private money on research, with about one-third of this going on basic and applied biomedical research. By 1990, industrially sponsored research, growing at 20 per cent per year, had outpaced the Ministry of Education's allocation and reached $461m (*Nature* 1990a). Red tape is reported to be a problem, and long periods elapse between university receipt of funds and researchers being able to access them.

In spite of current trends in industrial funding, Japanese academics have traditionally been even more reluctant than their western colleagues to become involved in industrial collaboration. Perhaps this has been owing to the fact that they are not allowed to do consultancy, or any other outside work. They are allowed to do sponsored research within the university, and there may be some element of indirect payment from companies such as travel money and generous expenses (Fransman 1990). They can also be seconded to the research institutes, or hold joint appointments in both organisations: this is the case with several senior staff at the National Institute for Basic Biology at Okazaki (NIBB 1988).

The organisation of university research does not fit very well with current ideas of what is optimal for basic research. The Professors control the research of their juniors, and they are themselves promoted for the most part on the basis of seniority. Interactions between groups may also be difficult. The possibility that these structural problems may be inhibiting good basic research has been extensively debated in Japan and there are moves to re-organise research groupings along American lines. The system has already been changed in some of the private universities (Fransman 1990).

The level of contract research sponsored by companies in the ninety-five national universities is not high – reports from the Science and Technology Agency (STA) and the Ministry of Education (MoE) give figures of 241 research contracts involving 154 companies and a small total sum of money (about £10m, no year given but probably after 1983).

There is also a programme of collaborative research between universities and companies where benefits are mutual and one-third of the funds come from the government. The total sums involved, including both the public and private contribution, were in the order of Y39m in each of 1984 and 1985.

Consultancy

Makoto Kikuchi, Sony's Managing Director, reports a successful inventing/consultancy arrangement (Phillips 1989). A Professor at Tohoku University who had worked with Sony engineers for many years had a novel idea for a 'perpendicular recording technique'. Taking the basis of this idea, Sony worked out a way to design a new type of recording head. The process of collaboration in this case was smooth and effective. Kikuchi believes that it is essential for this sort of co-operation to become much more common in Japan. However, he points to several problems:

1 University laboratories are underfinanced and inadequately equipped. This restricts the possibilities of research in some areas, including semiconductor technology.
2 Japanese companies are so competitive that there is no possibility that a university Professor will be allowed into most company labs. Academics are not sufficiently accustomed to the need for total confidentiality and in any case are not part of the organisation. Thus it is not possible for academics to acquire a deep understanding of a company's needs.

However, it has been suggested elsewhere that Japanese Professors' multiple consultancies for more than one company are actually an avenue of technology diffusion, in a society in which people rarely change jobs (Clark 1985).

Secondment of company scientists to universities

This service is reported to be highly regarded by participating companies as an effective training opportunity. Participants pay a small fee to the government.

Patent rights

In the case of contract research carried out in the national universities for external sponsors, the Japanese government takes ownership of any patent rights that arise. The sponsor or anyone he chooses to name has the first option to license the technology for up to 7 years after the research is completed, subject to payment of royalties. The situation is the same for collaborative research, except that the period of the licence is 5 years.

Similar rules are imposed in the other government-funded

research organisations. Private universities make their own arrangments as they see fit.

The national research institutes

The national research institutes, set up by the government to implement the R&D policies of the ministries and other public sector organisations, receive the bulk of central research funding. The main group are supported by a division of the Ministry of International Trade and Industry (MITI). They spend the lion's share of basic research funds, mainly on the physical sciences, although they also carry out some health sciences research. One of the oldest institutes, RIKEN, houses Japan's Human Genome Project and important genetic collections at its laboratories in Tsukuba Science City.

There is also a major new group, the National Institutes of Basic Biology in Okazaki, which is funded by Monbusho.

Collaborative projects

A number of programmes have been initiated, such as the Creative Science and Technology Promotion System, which are designed to address the perceived suppression of invention by the existing structures. They attempt to create different organisational and group structures within selected laboratories. The hope is that by setting up research groups that avoid the traditional Japanese social and work patterns, a more individualistic and creative atmosphere will be engendered which may encourage invention. The feeling is that from its position at the forefront of technology in several fields, Japan can no longer rely on others to supply the generic technologies. Many of these collaborative programmes include non-Japanese partners (Schmid 1991).

The government has also set up a number of special groups to foster western-style research patterns. ERATO (Exploratory Research for Advanced Technology) was set up in 1981 to sponsor 5-year research projects on 'blue skies' topics. They are staffed by younger researchers from companies and universities, sometimes including foreign workers, and they are more individualistic in style.

While officially supporting the need to expand basic research, the government has shown reluctance to expand research funding to anything like the levels of the USA or West Germany. In addition, the joint projects, which were supposed to have a more basic direction, are also reported to veer towards the applied in the same way as do other Japanese projects (Davis 1990).

There may be some success in the aim of promoting individualism. Fransman (1990) relates several cases where an influential individual determined the course of a joint research programme rather than the more frequently reported Japanese consensus-creating system. Fuchi, Chairman of the Basic Theory Group in the fifth-generation computer project, ICOT, pressed for the project to be based on non-von Neumann architectures. At that time (1981) only Fuchi and his group believed that knowledge information processing had a future. Fuchi used a Prolog program sent to him by researchers at Edinburgh, to demonstrate the suitability of Prolog as the key language for knowledge information processing. Electronics companies and some of MITI's engineers were against, but the Machinery and Information Industries Bureau supported Fuchi strongly. Three years later the firms were beginning to change their minds. Now both the firms and MITI believe that KIP will become steadily more important.

Hajime Kitakami of Fujitsu remarked to Fransman that it was very stimulating for him to have the opportunity to talk to world-class researchers when he visited foreign labs as an ICOT worker, rather than as a Fujitsu scientist. For Japanese scientists, ICOT is the place to go to find out everything that is happening in Japan and abroad. Company workers feel that the project has been very successful in generating new ideas and capabilities for innovation within their firms, although some report a degree of alienation from their previous colleagues.

In other MITI-directed collaborative projects, there is variation in the proportion of the research that is carried out co-operatively and that which is done separately, within company labs. A delicate balance is sought between competition and co-operation. One should, however, note Fransman's findings from a questionnaire survey of four major companies involved in supposedly collaborative projects to develop technology. He found that the firms considered that they had competed intensely in the course of developing the technologies. Another finding was that firms believed the main contribution the government had made was through the provision of subsidies for the research. They perceived that the main benefits for the company, apart from the financial aid, came from devoting additional corporate research attention to the technologies.

The point that additional corporate attention was directed at the technologies is very interesting. It implies that MITI played a role in spotting important new areas, later perceived by the companies to have been correct. Another important effect in Japan has been to permit a much wider diffusion of new technology than would have occurred spontaneously, given the 'bounded vision' of the organisations involved. Nevertheless, one aspect of Fransman's findings which is particularly relevant here is that there was very little true co-operation, with joint creation and sharing of knowledge.

How successful these programmes are is hotly debated. Companies are admitted both by MITI and by company representatives to be less than enthusiastic about joint projects. One criticism of ICOT was that it failed to produce anything fundamentally new. It has been counterargued that it was set up to do innovative, long-term, applied (not basic) research. This criticism of the lack of basic work is echoed implicitly by companies and scientists. Following the fifth-generation project, a new international institute is being set up, to start in 1992. It will explore the possibilities of neural, biological and optical computing. The initial sponsors are major companies. The aim is to be more flexible in approach, with more basic research and to encourage the involvement of foreign researchers.

Both the companies and the scientists involved at present are keen to avoid government support, at least in the first round. The implication is that government pressures for applications and 'Japan first' are seen as excessive by both scientists and private sector sponsors (*Nature* 1990b). Given the stated reluctance of companies to be involved in collaborations set up by MITI, one can only conclude that their lack of enthusiasm is confined to the near-market stages. For risky, long-term projects they may be more willing to accept the advantages of spreading the risks.

Evaluation of collaborative research projects

Evaluation of research, both basic and applied, is a topic which has provoked a great deal of discussion in Japan over the last ten years. There is felt to be a need for more effective methods, and new approaches are being tried.

In the joint government/industry programmes, targets are agreed before the project starts by the prolonged, consensus-seeking procedures used in Japanese organisations. The discussions involve the companies, the government agencies and laboratories. Evaluation is normally built into projects at the start. It is a routine part of research management (Irvine 1988). There is considerable emphasis on comparing technical outcomes with initial targets.

Independent assessment committees and external peer review are also regarded as useful by all participants, although this is unfamiliar to Japanese culture and still in the process of introduction. It is felt that this may contribute to the aim of increasing the creativity of Japanese research, by removing some of the bias towards conservatism.

Independent assessment of government research institutes is also being introduced. One study suggests that evaluation may contribute to more effective use of results (Kodama *et al.* 1981): 92 per cent of researchers from laboratories with evaluation systems believed their results were sufficiently used, compared with 79 per cent in laboratories which had not introduced evaluation. This same report found that research managers and researchers themselves must be fully aware of the need for research evaluation, and its efficacy, for it to be effective. This was accepted by the STA, which then decreed that evaluation methods must be introduced carefully and with full explanation so as to gain acceptance by the researchers (Irvine 1988). One point on which they were particularly insistent was that midterm and final assessments should be related to the initial plan. They believed that most assessment tasks can be undertaken internally, provided there is regular external assessment. This applied also to evaluation by the agencies of the programmes they support.

The rate of production of publications and patents is among the measures regarded as important. Counts of papers and conference presentations are used by both companies and government. For companies, rates of return on research investment are also considered to matter, although it is conceded that such figures are inaccurate (Irvine 1988). Government, on the other hand, is not concerned with short-term financial measures of success. It is placing increasing stress on the take-up of new technology by industry, especially by the participating companies.

Patenting and licensing

MITI retains ownership of the patents, and companies must pay (reduced) royalties for a licence; however they reckon that the know-how they gain developing technology as directed by MITI gives them a considerable edge, and this they do not surrender. Companies work separately under MITI direction when it comes to prototype development, and there is no co-operation at this point.

The Japan Industrial Technology Association (JITA) has the role of making the results of national institute R&D available to industry and of supporting interaction between industry and the institutes. JITA does not confine its activities to Japan. It presents the latest technology developed in the institutes to audiences overseas. It has a total of about 20,000 patents and technologies, of which about 2,500 have been licensed.

Japanese companies in international collaborations

Japanese industry is not investing solely in Japanese science: companies are spending lavishly abroad on basic research projects. They have taken with enthusiasm to collaborative relationships with western universities, and with small, R&D-based companies that maintain close academic links. The electronics giant NEC has set up a research institute in the USA at Princeton to accommodate work in areas which it hopes will ultimately assist development of new products such as the 'interpretation telephone', which will translate automatically. Hitachi has extended its R&D network to Dublin, Cambridge (England), California and Michigan, where it has set up laboratories.

The cosmetics giant Shiseido gave £60m to set up a Cutaneous Biology Research Center with Harvard Medical Center and Massachusetts General Hospital to carry out skin research. Kobe Steel gave North Carolina State University $400,000 for a chair to study electronic materials. It is also pursuing a number of joint electronics research projects in British universities, and recently (1990) increased this commitment by establishing a laboratory on Surrey Research Park to work on polymers and diamond thin films for the next generation of electronic integrated circuits. The pharmaceutical companies Eisai and Yamanouchi have both set up research institutes on UK campuses.

These are just a few of the many significant investments that Japanese companies in a range of industries have made in western, university-based science.

WEST GERMANY

In West Germany (unification is so recent that only the situation before that date is considered here), basic research on a broad scale, applied research and technology development are all believed to underpin innovation (Goerdeler 1985). This view is implemented through basic research programmes carried out in the universities, the Max Planck Institutes and industry sector research institutes (Redwood 1991; CEST 1991).

Funding involves a mix of federal, state and private contributions. West Germany also participates in the EC joint programmes, but not as wholeheartedly as the UK and France (Arnold and Guy 1986).

Fraunhofer Institutes

The Fraunhofer Institutes in particular are dedicated to working at the interface between industry and universities and are the main location for formal, contract research and development. They also offer technological information and advisory services (FHG 1988). Initially heavily supported by government, they have been so successful that they are now funded on the basis that they receive an equal contribution from the state for everything they get from industry. Thus industry's costs are 50 per cent of project cost (Roericht 1985).

The institutes are on university premises and can use young university personnel. Senior engineers and scientists in the institutes have normally worked for 10–15 years in industry or a government agency after getting their doctorates. When they come back to work in the institute, they have extensive experience and contacts in industry. At present, however, it is proving difficult to attract people back from industry (Roericht 1985). Professors maintain a joint appointment with a university, thus keeping a tight linkage between university/institute/industry. Informal relationships reinforce this: industry managers, academics and bank managers are reported to get together at the local Chamber of Commerce for a drink after work (Simon Harris, personal communication).

The universities

The universities are generously funded, mainly by the *Länder* (states). The emphasis is on the obligation of the university towards companies. Companies have the right to use all information systems and other facilities at no or marginal cost. Professors are paid privately by companies to do research for them, in their own laboratories. They use some of the money to pay for any additional expense that this causes, but keep most of it as a consultancy fee.

There are some constraints. Universities are legally obliged to publish and cannot enter into agreements which preclude this. However they can permit delays of 2–12 months.

Brokering

There are many other organisations to support technology transfer, drawing their funds from governmental sources at all levels and also from Chambers of Commerce. AGIT, an intermediary or broker whose task is to link universities and other research centres with small and medium firms in North Rhine/Westphalia is one of many such (Redwood 1991).

This brokering function is perceived to be particularly important in effecting linkages between higher education institutions and industry. It is widely recognised that serious barriers exist to such relationships and that special organisations are required as intermediaries between the parties.

Effectiveness

The German system recognises that different mechanisms are required to serve different functions in the spectrum of relationships between basic or applied workers and small, medium and large companies. It accepts that creating good channels of communication is essential, and tries to achieve this by whatever appear to be the most effective means. There is no attempt to standardise according to a narrow model.

In spite of this, the system is not regarded as entirely satisfactory by the participants. All funds are subject to the same massive bureaucratic regulation, regardless of whether they originate from the public or private sector. This is the case even where the private sector is the dominant source of support. At Aachen in 1985, for instance, some laboratories were earning up to 85 per cent of their equipment and running costs from industry. This was not atypical (Roericht 1985). Companies complain about the institutional inflexibility and threaten to go elsewhere.

Nevertheless, the fact that the many programmes for technology transfer are supported mainly by industry argues that they have been of great benefit to the industrial sector (Redwood 1991). This is borne out by the high level of importance attributed to them by senior German executives in a recent survey of sources of technology carried out by the English Centre for Exploitation of Science and Technology (CEST 1991).

FRANCE

France provides very substantial governmental funding for research and development over a wide range of basic and applied science and technologies. Research is carried out both in higher education institutions and in government research institutes. Until recently both the direction of research and technology transfer were fairly centralised, but there has been a determined and effective drive to create a network of regional centres.

There have also been a number of successful local initiatives to improve the efficiency of commercialisation. The special programmes and courses in high technology entrepreneurship set up by the Ecole Supérieure de Commerce de Lyon are an excellent example. These courses are aimed primarily at scientists and engineers working in research institutes and large companies who are interested in setting up their own companies. Between 1985 and 1990, twenty-one companies had been started by participants, which have so far had a very low failure rate by national standards (Albert et al. 1990). The initial training courses are backed up by continuing support from the Centre des Entrepreneurs at ESC Lyon.

Most of the regions have comprehensive programmes for economic development which include frameworks for joint university/ industry projects linked to the economic needs of the area. The Regional Council of Brittany in 1989 set up an agency, BRITTA, to co-ordinate a comprehensive array of services and financial aids to support technology transfer into local industry, specifically for biotechnology which is regarded as particularly important in an area with a large food industry. Its offerings include grants to help fund joint research between institutes and companies, financial assistance to acquire licences and know-how, and many other inducements to encourage development of a local, high technology, bioscience-based industry. There is also active encouragement of inward investment in the region. Subsidiaries of foreign firms share in the entitlement to assistance.

Government research institutes

CNRS

The Centre National de la Recherche Scientifique (CNRS) carries out 20 per cent of French public research in its 1,300 laboratories. Its mission is fundamental research, but it must take the needs of industry into account. Industry in this case is defined as French enterprises, or foreign-owned companies which provide employment, preferably in R&D, in France (Duby 1985).

The centre organises 'clubs' which bring together its own researchers with members from several companies, usually large, to look at specific technological problems. It sometimes seconds researchers to industry for 1–2 years: two-thirds return to CNRS, and one-third remain with the company. It requires that research projects must be of basic scientific interest as well as industrial interest.

CNRS will patent and license its own technology. It also has funds and facilities to carry out predevelopment work. It apportions a share of royalties to the inventor and to the individual laboratory.

INSERM

The Institut National de la Santé et de la Recherche Médicale (INSERM) has 250 research centres concerned with medical, biomedical and public health research. Recently it has added a responsibility to assist in setting up companies to its traditional roles of training, research, consultancy and dissemination of knowledge (INSERM 1991).

Technology transfer organisations

ANVAR

The Agence Nationale de la Valorisation de la Recherche (ANVAR) is the main central government organisation with responsibility for technology transfer. It has twenty-two regional offices to advise and help firms. Its main objectives are to encourageage industrial innovation, to evaluate research work carried out in universities and institutes, and to help industry to access the international markets. It plays an important role as broker between companies and French public sector research workers. It will look abroad for licensees of French inventions and is currently very actively promoting international joint ventures (ANVAR 1989). It is proud of its record in assisting smaller companies and claims to have aided more than 13,000 French companies.

CRITT

In the course of the last few years, the regions have been encouraged to set up their own centres for innovation and technology transfer (CRITT). These are beginning to play an important role in liaising between local industry and higher education centres, and in offering information services, consultancy and financial support. They are closely geared to the needs of the local economy and most support is contingent on a substantial share of costs being borne by the participating companies.

They and ANVAR also advise companies and research laboratories about participation in EC research and development programmes.

International collaboration

France was for a long time extremely nationalistic in its policies for supporting high technology. Substantial government-backed projects in a wide range of technologies were initiated in the 1960s and 1970s. Their highly interventionist approach was intensified in 1981. The incoming socialist administration carried out a massive nationalisation programme which put 25 per cent of manufacturing industry in government hands (Stoffaes 1984). This was followed by corporate restructuring planned to strengthen French computer and telecommunications technology (Arnold and Guy 1986).

Since 1982 the policies have tried to treat individual industries as a series of networks of supplier/user relationships, and have attempted to intervene in ways that would have positive, knock-on effects throughout the industry (Dang Nguyen, Gaudefroy and Arnold 1985). A number of major programmes have been set up to boost French technological competitiveness, but the escalating costs and lack of success of many of the major firms have diminished enthusiasm for this approach. In France, as in the UK, there is increasing emphasis on European collaborative programmes (Arnold and Guy 1986).

EUROPEAN COMMISSION JOINT RESEARCH PROJECTS

In the early 1980s, Europe's performance in high technology industries was poor. 'National champions' dominated the protected, national markets. Morale was low and European firms were suffering a crisis of confidence in their own capabilities. The problems were due to management failure rather than to any lack of technology. Viscount Davignon, EC Commissioner for Industry, Research and Technology, persuaded the Commission to set up a collaborative R&D programme, along the lines which had apparently been successful for MITI in Japan.

The first programme was ESPRIT, the European Strategic Programme for Research in Information Technology, initiated in 1984. The funds came equally from the Community and from the companies involved. A total of 200m ecus per annum was spent in the first phase, followed by 400m ecus. Projects were planned to be industry-led, for the most part. Recently there has been some strong questioning of the effectiveness of the ESPRIT programme, some of it emanating from Brussels (de Jonquières 1990). A *Nature* editorial article (1990c) remarked that much of the work was excellent, and that those involved had gained much greater competence in their daily business. However, it concluded that it would be more effective for the EC to spend more on higher education and research than on transnational projects.

Margaret Sharp (1989) believes that ESPRIT has been of great importance for several reasons. The first is that projects were not planned centrally: bids were solicited in broadly defined areas, allowing companies to decide what they proposed to do. This resembles the system for awarding research grants to UK and US university scientists. It was also accompanied by a review process which involved special teams, some seconded from industry, whose role was to select, monitor and facilitate the progress of projects.

Another point which Sharp makes in favour of ESPRIT was its confidence-boosting effect. The rapid growth in privately sponsored joint ventures and, increasingly, in mergers, which started in the mid-1980s, may have been triggered to some extent by ESPRIT, which provided a mechanism and channel of co-operation, and established a common framework of expectations among key decision-makers. She suggests that it also created a major lobby in favour of completing the internal market (the 1992 process). The joint framework also has the effect of creating standards, a feature of Japanese collaborations which has been recommended. However, the explosion of mergers has not won such support in all quarters. Other commentators have been less sanguine.

While it is often stated that the EC collaborative programmes are ill-designed to permit smaller firms to participate, ESPRIT's first phase appears to have involved a fair number of smaller organisations (Hare *et al.* 1989): 17.3 per cent were smaller than 50 (employees), 22.2 per cent had 51–500 employees and they attracted 19.7 per cent of the funding, compared with 23.3 per cent to universities, 17.1 per cent to medium-to-large and 20.1 per cent to large. Given that large firms were often involved in more than one project and contributed more resources, this does not seem a poor representation of small firms. However, smaller organisations had significantly fewer contracts than would have been predicted on the basis of their representation in the UK company sector (Hare *et al.* 1989).

EUREKA, seen by some as an answer to the US Strategic Defense Initiative (SDI), although not defence oriented, covered a range of technologies and was not limited to precompetitive research, but also included collaborative product development. The EUREKA High Definition Television (HDTV) project seems to be collapsing in the wake of the BSB/Sky Television merger. It includes seven non-EC European countries. It is funded mainly by the member countries, although the EC contributes some funds as well.

ESPRIT has been succeeded by an array of programmes with names like BRITE, SPRITE, FLAIR and ECLAIR, covering a wide range of technologies. The format is similar to that of ESPRIT. The sums of money involved are large. In all cases, industry puts up 50 per cent of the costs, academic research partners have their running costs covered, and any one project must have participants from more than one EC country. The IPR belongs equally to all participants.

CURRENT TRENDS

The most striking fact to emerge from this international comparison is that the Japanese success in microelectronics was built on a foundation of closely managed, in-house innovation in large companies. This was supported by a centrally controlled, economic environment which offered favourable conditions to these companies. While some co-operation in research and development was orchestrated by the government, it appears that a high level of competition between domestic rivals always existed.

In the period when Japan was building its powerful position in this industry, Japanese basic research and government funding were not an important factor. Now that Japan is at the forefront of technology in this and several related areas, the Japanese are moving towards the idea that they will have to generate a greater body of fundamental research themselves to underpin future developments.

While Japanese companies and academics themselves are showing a desire to escape from the surveillance of the Japanese government, and to arrange collaborative projects with a less immediate market focus, the rest of the world appears to be moving towards more extensive government or supranational collaboration. Widespread fear of the Japanese competitive threat and the vast costs of the projects is pushing governments of other industrialised countries into Japanese-style, government-co-ordinated programmes. It is far from clear that this approach will achieve its objective of enhancing competitiveness through improving the precompetitive technology base. On the surface, at least, there appears to be a tendency for some of the larger European and American companies to use these collaborations as a means to create a quasi-monopolistic position, then to demand protection from foreign competition. The fierce internal competition which characterises the Japanese electronics industry has been avoided.

The technological successes of the recent past in the USA have had a very different pattern from Japan's. Small companies exploiting campus-derived technology have been an important element in America's economic vitality. In Germany too, which in Europe has had the most success in developing a buoyant technologically advanced industrial base since the war, small and medium-sized companies have played an important part in generating this economic vitality. Thus it is by no means clear that attempting to emulate the pattern which worked for Japan in the past, with its peculiar corporate characteristics, will achieve similar results for western countries with very different histories and social structures.

While there has been some lip-service paid in Europe to the importance of creating new companies as part of the push towards technological leadership, the French and British programmes and also the EC joint programmes have had little success in involving small companies. Where they have, the small participants have complained about large-company dominance. There is a need to consider the special needs of small companies operating in an environment that is designed for large firms, which is the case in much of Europe, and which is increasingly true of the EC as a whole. If, indeed, the creation and growth of new companies play an important role in generating European vitality in high technology areas, this question must be addressed.

It is by no means clear, in any case, that American and European loss of competitiveness is due to failures at the level addressed by the government-co-ordinated programmes – the level of precompetitive research. These areas have always been much more heavily funded in the west than in Japan, and with a high degree of success. It is remarked again and again in many quarters that Japanese success is a function of close concentration on manufacturing efficiency, on firm control of suppliers, and of tightly managed innovation with very precise market objectives. To compete here requires the hard slog of rationalising businesses, improving skills, cutting unnecessary costs and improving general management. These less glamorous tactics are being advocated increasingly in highly influential quarters in the USA and Europe (Dertouzos 1989; NEDO 1990). The need to stay at the forefront in terms of development, acquisition and effective use of technology is one of the central recommendations of these commentators, but the focus is on the individual firm's competitiveness, rather than the nation's. This has the appeal of the possible, where vast national and supranational projects have no great history of success in the west.

This is not to say that the great, collaborative projects have failed to meet some of their objectives. The final report on the Alvey Programme (Guy *et al.* 1991) commends it for having developed a collaborative culture which was sorely needed. In particular, it comments that academic/industrial collaboration was successful, and that the ability of academics to respond to industrial priorities improved over time. Thus these projects have created a more friendly environment for future joint activities. It may well be that the facilitation of companies' access to academic researchers is the most significant outcome affecting future competitiveness. This, at least, is a definite improvement in the efficient use of scarce resources. It also plays to the strengths of western societies, with their notable capacity for invention.

One must hope that the current focus on major international collaborations among companies will not distract attention from the need for better innovation management at the later stages of product development. Nor should it be permitted to obscure the very real internal barriers to innovation within many European countries.

The next two chapters analyse several of the factors that continue to block the smooth diffusion of new technology from the university or small company inventor to the marketplace in the UK. The problems of managing the interface between culturally different organisations is discussed. There are threats but also opportunities for the large company. The general environment for innovation in Britain offers different possibilities which many companies now find attractive.

Chapter 7

The university and the company – different cultures

From this survey of technology transfer from universities to industry two key issues emerge. One is how far it is possible to generalise from past experience and from the experience of other countries. What is it permissible to conclude from such disparate data, collected over many years and in more than one country? An issue which is even more fundamental, however, is that of the role of the university in society. What is this role, and does it include crucially important functions which are not in the long term compatible with the demands of direct university/company technology transfer? In this chapter this latter issue is addressed, and implications are drawn for the types of interactions that will be most fruitful for both companies and universities.

THE ORGANISATIONAL SPECTRUM

Universities and companies differ in several significant ways. While they do not all fall neatly into one of two categories, individual organisations can be assigned to approximate positions on a continuum of organisational types, as shown in Figure 7.1. This places general universities at one end and large companies at the other.

The continuum passes from general universities, through technical universities, then to research institutes. These show considerable individual differences in the extent to which they are required to meet applied, industrially relevant objectives, and to collaborate with companies. The trajectory carries on through small companies with one foot in the university, and ultimately to large companies with entirely commercial objectives.

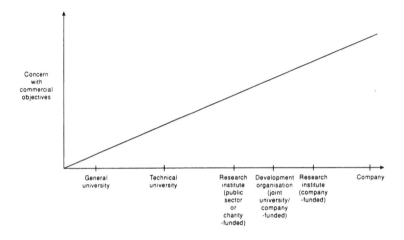

Figure 7.1   The cultural continuum from university to company

THE OBJECTIVES AND ORGANISATION OF THE UNIVERSITY

Let us consider the main objectives of organisations at the general university end of the spectrum.

The formal roles

Universities have a major responsibility for carrying out formal programmes of higher education and professional training. This obligation is closely linked to their role as repositories for the accumulated knowledge base of their disciplines. Since the early years of this century this has increasingly been interpreted to include a responsibility for carrying out basic research in the sciences. This is the function of generating new knowledge.

The outputs which universities are now universally expected to generate are trained manpower, and 'new knowledge', disseminated freely in the form of learned papers, conference communications, and the like. These are the uncontroversial core activities of modern universities. Their unifying characteristic is that the university's responsibilities are towards society as a whole, rather than to individual interest groups. The collective knowledge and expertise of the university is at the service of mankind. A point to note is that the fulfilment of these responsibilities places a low priority on meeting deadlines. 'Understanding', 'reliability', 'significance', are some of the terms which describe the ethos of the approach.

As we move along the continuum from 'general university', there is a progressive reduction in the universe addressed by the university, limited first by national then regional boundaries, and gradually acquiring more specific economic obligations towards particular sectors such as agriculture, medicine or engineering. But the emphasis continues to be on openness.

The less formalised functions

There is also an array of linked activities and outputs from most universities which differ qualitatively from the primary, formal aims, and which give rise to conflict and disagreement both within the university and beyond its walls. They include:

1 Dissemination of knowledge and expertise of members of staff through paid consultancy, often involving production of confidential reports.
2 As above, with the appointment of a member of staff to a directorship in a company.
3 Applied research projects carried out under contract for commercial organisations, often with some requirements for confidentiality.
4 Involvement of university in exploitation of technology invented by members of staff in the course of their research.
5 Involvement of individual members of staff in setting up a company to exploit their research.

All these activities contravene the primary requirement for free dissemination of information. The outputs generated benefit narrow interest groups, usually single commercial organisations. They also compete for scarce resources which might otherwise be used to generate more of the uncontroversial outputs.

Why have universities become involved in activities that appear to be incompatible with their primary purposes? This situation has evolved under the pressure of many social and economic demands. A great deal of acrimonious debate has accompanied their increasing prominence among university activities. The history and current state of this debate in the UK and the USA is discussed in Chapters 2 to 4. In this chapter we will confine ourselves to considering the issues to emerge as a function of this internal incompatibility of objectives, and the implications for companies interacting with universities.

The reward system of academics

The reward system is tied very closely to the formal teaching and basic research functions of the university, with heaviest emphasis on the basic research performance (Merton 1973; Gaston 1978). A common complaint is that academics pay insufficient attention to their teaching, and that promotion is earned only by research eminence. However, academics are usually required to carry out a certain amount of teaching as a condition of their employment. When the scheduled time for a lecture arrives, research and other activities must be abandoned and the teaching commitment fulfilled. Teaching in the form of supervision of postgraduate research, or serving as external examiner in other universities, are definite pluses for the curriculum vitae. Thus teaching is usually a *sine qua non* for promotion. Nevertheless the quality and quantity of academics' teaching is not yet generally subjected to systematic assessment and is thus not of great importance for career advancement.

Promotion within the university system and general professional success for academic scientists and technologists is in most cases more directly tied to quality and quantity of publications in academic journals, and measures of academic esteem such as rate of citation of publications, invitations to give papers at academic meetings, organise colloquia, etc. Publications in professional magazines and confidential consultancy reports are not reckoned to be of value (THES 1991) for academic rewards, and must be prepared at the expense of time which could be devoted to 'purer' academic pursuits.

This appears to indicate a fairly straightforward route to success. In order to achieve rapid promotion, the academic ought to perform a minimum of teaching and disseminate research findings through all the academically approved media. Other activities will simply detract from this. Why then should the academic threaten a promising career by developing relationships with industry? The answer, of course, has to do with the inputs that both the university and the academic require in order to achieve these approved academic outputs.

Funding academia

The possibility of carrying out research in science and technology is dependent on obtaining considerable financial support. Universities have variable levels of internal resources for these purposes. Governments and charitable foundations also make very substantial funds available. However, the supply of funds available for basic research never meets the demand. Thus academic scientists are often obliged to consider applying to companies for research support. Since companies are unlikely to be interested in curiosity-driven research as such, a research project must be planned which has general scientific significance but also involves creating some new technology or body of knowledge which could have commercial value to a company. If this compromise can be achieved, funds may be awarded by a company to the academic to carry out the research. This is not always as difficult as it sounds. Many fields of scientific research contain extensive areas which are of mutual interest to companies and to basic researchers, although the nature of the interest of each party is quite different.

This situation, in which a project of genuine mutual interest receives industrial funding, usually has strong institutional support, since here the interests of the academic and of the institution are at one. It should be noted, however, that the element of compromise may create problems for the relationship with the company if it is not acknowledged and dealt with. It is unlikely that the project can be designed so that it is entirely satisfactory to all parties.

Individual financial rewards

Where other activities involving academics and companies are concerned, the institution's position may be somewhat ambivalent. For example, where a common area of interest exists, the scientist's expertise may be valuable to the company on a consultancy basis. Since academics' salaries are not particularly generous, a consultancy fee may be welcome. The return to the institution from this transaction is often less clear. Some insist that academic consultancy must be carried out through the university, which then takes part of the fee. This is not always the case, however, and it is difficult to enforce even where it is the rule.

Taking things a step further, the scientist in the course of basic research may develop new techniques which can be perceived to have possible commercial applications. While the institution will not offer career rewards for success in commercialisation, the process may yield financial returns to both the inventor and the institution.

However, no matter how greatly these financial rewards are appreciated, the opportunity cost is the time and energy which could have been spent by the scientist on pursuing academic career objectives. The total returns to the institution are difficult to assess, since they include benefits in terms of contacts, future career opportunities for graduates, and other indirect returns which are hard to measure. They are not always perceived by the university to be adequate and conflicts of interest are often created. These conflicts must be addressed by the institutions, the academics, and their industrial collaborators, in order to understand how to organise effective interaction. The formulas which have been reached by many American and British universities in order to minimise the problems were discussed in detail in Chapters 2 to 4.

The organisation of the university community

Another key difference between universities and companies is the looseness of organisation and lack of formal reporting structures in universities compared with companies.

An academic's success is very individual, tied closely to his or her personal name and its fame in the professional world. A successful academic with a constellation of graduate students, research assistants and visitors from other institutions may have a very ill-defined relationship with the institution. The prestige of the individual, his or her external support systems and responsibilities to the professional world of science give a position of power in dealings with the institution, which needs for the sake of its own standing to have prestigious academics associated with it.

Often much of the academic's income comes from external sources, which further dilutes the hold of the institution. This is often a matter of university policy. Many American universities employ their permanent staff on 10-month contracts. The expectation is that they will find 2 months' salary elsewhere, either from research grants or from summer school teaching. In both the USA and Britain many institutions also actively encourage staff to undertake a certain amount of paid consultancy work, for the sake of the links it forges with other organisations. The power relationships within the university are thus very nebulous, especially to external organisations.

Even the young, less-established academic will be expected to exercise a degree of autonomy about the content and mode of pursuit of his or her work, which is very different from the position of a middle-level executive in most companies. While some companies are trying to create a looser type of organisation, with more decentralisation of control and more participative styles of management, this is still a far cry from the degree of freedom enjoyed by most academics in their work. In fact, the management style of the university scientist with his or her team probably bears more resemblance to the entrepreneur with a small start-up company than to that of a departmental or division manager in a big company.

THE COMPANY PERSPECTIVE

Company objectives are probably never quite as simple and straightforward as the Chairman's statements claim. However, compared with universities, they are relatively simple and comprehensible. Many universities' charters require the institution to operate for the 'good of mankind' and to perform other equally indefinable tasks. Companies are not burdened with such awkward formal obligations.

Then there is the agency problem. Organisational structures within western companies are usually fairly comprehensible and indicate with some accuracy the power relationships and the channels of command and communication. Doubtless these never work to perfection, but in general there is some correspondence between the official order and the way the system operates. Managers operating in this environment find it hard to understand the relationship of the academic scientist with the university's Director of Industrial Liaison and other administrators with whom the company manager involved in a joint project will have contact. Who controls whom and what? The answers have not always been clarified by the institution itself.

Controlling time horizons

Companies' R&D is on the whole directed towards fairly specific product or process developments, and there will usually be definite time horizons associated with a given project. For instance, the company may plan to replace aging production facilities in 3 years, and may wish to develop the control systems or some novel process to be implemented at that date. Keeping to a time schedule is imperative and a number of staff usually work on a single project full-time.

University scientists are in general more concerned to keep on exploring new ideas than to complete a given project on time. If an interesting finding takes them off in an unplanned direction, they are reluctant to be brought back on course. In addition, the joint project is probably competing with teaching and other research commitments for their time and attention. It may not necessarily have the highest priority.

Academics can also show extreme urgency in directions which are inconvenient for the company. If there is an exciting result, they want to publish it without delay. Secrecy may be crucial to the company's competitive edge, and to protect the right to patent.

FRUITFUL INTERACTION

Why become involved in a joint project with so many potential pitfalls? Most of the problems are now well recognised, and means have been evolved to minimise them. But they do still create difficulties. For this reason it is important for companies to recognise the types of projects which can be pursued more effectively in collaboration with universities than elsewhere, what should be avoided, and how to manage these collaborations when they do appear to offer the best alternative.

How the university science base can contribute

On a practical level, how can a company assess the opportunities for R&D risk reduction which company/campus relationships might offer it? The first step is to consider what the organisation's needs are, both immediately and in the longer term. The next is to look at the ways in which other companies have successfully addressed similar needs in the framework of a campus relationship.

Companies are succesfully using campus partnerships in several ways:

1 To access new technology.
2 To keep abreast of new developments and to access consultancy skills.
3 To develop new technology jointly.

They are also using the indirect route of joint venture with small, campus-linked technology companies as a way of accessing campus technology.

In the case of (1) – accessing technology which is to be developed entirely in-house – the primary requirements are for good information about the whereabouts of research programmes which might generate suitable inventions, and the whereabouts of recognised inventions. This involves scanning the scientific literature and appropriate databases, and sending R&D personnel to conferences to keep in touch with the work that is going on in university laboratories. If this is not possible, brokers such as the BTG can be consulted about the availability of new technology.

For (2) – keeping abreast of new developments – attendance at conferences, scanning the literature and maintaining a close relationship with a university close to the company's R&D laboratories are again the principal requirements.

For (3), relationships must be taken a step further, and it may be difficult to locate a suitable partner who is conveniently close to a company facility. This is the point at which definite commitments must be considered. This may involve significant internal management changes to deal with the interfacing problems that arise in a continuing interaction with an external group. This may raise cultural problems which are difficult to overcome, or which can be more easily dealt with in the context of a direct relationship with a small company, which itself handles the interface with the academics.

This last course may be chosen because the small company is already in the process of developing an interesting piece of technology: the indirect relationship the large company then has with academia is coincidental. In this case, both companies can benefit from the university expertise, but the small company must handle the interaction. If the company is looking for a source of novel technology which will strengthen its product and process range in the medium to longer term, it might prefer to develop a continuing relationship with a good laboratory which is not already heavily involved with other corporate sponsors.

Basic research is still a growth area, and new research groups are constantly being set up. Younger scientists developing a career often choose to go to a less famous institution where they can command more favourable conditions for their research work. Consequently good science is by no means exclusively the province of the most prestigious academic institutions. This early career stage is also the point at which researchers without pre-established corporate links are keenest to establish relationships, to underpin their efforts. It is a good stage for a company to start a relationship which it hopes will steadily contribute to its specialist research needs.

Where a very specific research project is required, then a direct contract with a university-based scientist whose expertise is most appropriate is the means to employ. Where the objectives are broader (i.e. keeping close to new technology, potential manpower, maintaining company awareness of recent research), association with a development organisation on campus is probably the best route. Other companies may already be sponsoring the organisation, but this need not necessarily exclude new entrants. This lacks the complete exclusivity of a contractual relationship with one laboratory, but usually there will still be limitations on the dissemination of the more commercialisable IPR. The organisation will usually be set up to serve multiple objectives.

Not all interactions with academics require long preparations and cautious assessment. Where a company is looking for expert advice from the acknowledged leader in a field, a limited piece of consulting work can be commissioned. There may be some competition for the authority's services. The price may be quite high, and the availability restricted. The expert will usually, however, have a greater fund of experience of working with industry than the younger researcher. This will be likely to enhance the effectiveness of the interaction. On the other hand, sometimes the expert is in fact both young and inexperienced in consultancy, and there may be considerable communication difficulties.

No matter what types of service the company is looking for, there will also be the decision to stay local or to go to the best available internationally. Again, this will depend on exactly what the company wants from the interaction. Modern communications make distance less of a barrier, but language and culture can still create problems. For a large company, the answer might be to site a small R&D laboratory near to the academic centre with which contact is sought. This is a common practice, usually after there have been some preliminary interactions in the form of collaborative research projects.

Making the decision

A fair amount of effort should be invested in gathering and analysing information before deciding whether, and how, to initiate contact with a scientist or an organisation. It is also important to find out about both the organisation and the key individual scientists before making a final decision. There is an abundance of information sources, but they are not all particularly easy to use. Some important sources are listed in the Appendix, with brief descriptions. They are just a few of the multitude of organisations, databases, etc. which may be of use.

After doing the preliminary desk research, it is advisable to visit a few selected institutions and scientists to confirm impressions. The individual(s) who are expected to work at the academic/industrial interface must be included at this stage. They should certainly have established some personal contact with the academics they may have to work with, prior to negotiating any contracts. These personal relationships will be the key to the success of the interaction. If the individuals concerned have difficulty communicating within the framework that is set, and are unable to establish mutual trust, the collaboration is unlikely to succeed (Jenkins 1988).

Choosing the route

Where a company has limited resources and there is no appropriate local source of academic expertise, the use of a technology broker may be indicated. The technology brokers may in any case be the university's favoured agents for exploitation of a major invention, and consequently an early port of call for large companies as well. As Reimers has remarked (Reimers 1980), the expertise and resources required to effectively patent and protect important inventions worldwide is beyond the means of most university technology licensing offices. There will be substantial expenditure in the several years before royalty income builds up.

If the problems of communicating directly with the academic world are too great, the way forward may be through involvement with a campus-derived company which retains links itself with university research. Particularly as an initial step, this may feel more comfortable to the participants.

The small company route may also be the most appropriate in other contexts Where an exclusive relationship for a specific development is required, it should be considered. Monsanto, in collaboration with Oxford University and Raymond Dwek, has chosen this (see Chapter 3) as the means to commercialise Dwek's work on glycobiology. Much of the preliminary research was supported by Monsanto, and this represents a natural progression where a more commercial focus is needed, along with greater confidentiality and more commitment from the scientists.

This type of arrangement can permit an academic to make a more formal commitment to the commercialisation, while still retaining close academic links. It has the advantage of allowing all parties to reconsider at a later date whether the scientist wishes, or is suited, to a continuing corporate role. It retains the option of a return to full-time academic life, perhaps still carrying out consultancy for the company, or acting as a board member for the small company.

The small company option keeps open several possible avenues for the sponsoring firm. There are a number of points in the development at which it can choose whether to increase or reduce its commitment to the project, before any need for major decisions arrives. At the same time, its option to develop the technology is highly protected, and it will usually have considerable input to the development process in matters affecting the ultimate commerciality of the product.

Even if other contacts have been made, there are obvious advantages to maintaining links with an institution which is geographically close to the company's own base. This can be achieved by linking up with a nearby institution, if it has suitable expertise and facilities. Alternatively, the company may contemplate setting up an R&D facility on the science park of an institution with which it wishes to cultivate links. While strong arguments are made for keeping the company's R&D function close to the main decision-making centre, for many companies there is also an imperative to maintain R&D establishments close to centres of science expertise in several places or countries. Most science parks will have a number of tenants in this category. Heriot-Watt includes Syntex, Millipore and BBN, all headquartered in the USA, among its campus companies.

Developing informal local links can also be a useful first step, before making any firm commitment to a specific project. There need be little cost and no obligations attached to this educational experience. It is, in any case, the easiest way of keeping technical staff abreast of developments in their field.

THE MAIN PITFALLS

One of the commonest causes of dissatisfaction in university/industry interactions is the failure to meet expectations which were not mutually understood. It is essential at the outset of a relationship for the parties to be clear in their own minds and towards one another about their expectations of the project. Each should be clear about the constraints and the degrees of freedom for both sides. And these parameters should be decided with an understanding of how the best value can be obtained for each: spelling out to the last word the requirements on the university scientist will not elicit the most creative contribution. The project should be allowed some freedom to 'self-design' (Benassi 1991), since if the company could precisely spell out the route to follow, there would be no need to contract out. Limits to freedom of enquiry must be set, however, and good reporting systems are essential. This should be established at the outset in the legal agreement (Jenkins 1988).

To develop communication between industry and university scientists necessitates close interaction. Development organisations whose links with university departments and personnel are too tenuous are best avoided. A poorly organised interface may only distance the partners. The company is well advised to proceed cautiously. If in doubt, it is better to take one of the steps that delay commitment. The best relationships are built up step by step. In the long-term, a very significant level of commitment must be made by the company if these links are to play an effective role in its R&D strategy, but there is no advantage to be gained by making hasty decisions.

THE PROJECT PORTFOLIO RISK PROFILE

On the positive side, university liaison has a great deal to offer the R&D Director. Keeping all new project risk in-house is becoming more and more difficult in all high technology industries. It makes sense to hedge the risk by externalisation. The campus/company collaboration offers attractive possibilities for accessing state-of-the-art technology while retaining considerable flexibility in allocation of resources.

THE CONSEQUENCES FOR LONG-TERM PLANNING

The impact on corporate strategy is to allow a greater flexibility of choices. The company can take an option on a variety of very novel ideas and technologies, leaving final decisions about which to carry through to a later stage. Unlike in-house developments, there are unlikely to be complications due to internal politics and personal identification with a particular project which might interfere with objective choices. There is, however, some inevitable loss of control by the company.

INTERNATIONALISATION

How acceptable is this when the sponsoring company is headquartered in another country? The foreign company is securing the benefit of a collaboration at marginal cost. This is causing increasing political problems, particularly in the USA. The situation creates an uncomfortable dilemma, since much university-derived technology would not be developed at all if it were not for such international support. On the other hand, the investment of large amounts of state and federal money in the institutions and in basic research projects generates a demand that the benefits should not be reaped by economic competitors who do not offer any reciprocal source of new technology to the USA. No satisfactory answer to this debate has yet been found.

Many institutions in the USA address this by strongly favouring collaboration with companies that have a substantial, bona fide manufacturing presence in the USA (Sproull 1985). This is not required in the UK where there are no formal, and apparently no informal barriers to such collaborations.

ADVANTAGES FOR INDUSTRY

The costs of a given collaboration are usually moderate and controllable: universities are not profit-making; surplus cash goes mainly into improving research and library facilities and training of personnel, which returns added value to the sponsor.

There is a high degree of flexibility – it is easier to cancel projects and there is no long-term commitment to personnel, but returns are maximised by developing relationships over a period of time. This removes the communication difficulties inherent in the contrasting cultures and educates both parties in realistic expectations. Thus this should not be regarded as a cheap, short-term solution to the problems of strategic planning. Significant investment in the relationship is required to yield significant returns. It can only be used effectively in the context of a well thought-out, long-term strategy which clearly defines the areas of expertise which the company must maintain in-house. The ability effectively to integrate externalised R&D with in-house activities requires a significant commitment of resources, which is itself part of the investment in the relationship.

There is improved access to skills and facilities which could not be justified in-house, or which are better tested and considered before in-house commitment is reached. There is also a need for people to fill the interfacing roles – technology brokers or company and university personnel.

REQUIREMENTS

To optimise the university/industry interaction, there is a growing consensus about the conditions that must be created by both partners.

On the university side

It is essential that the institution should have decided what it wants from its programme of industrial liaison, and that it put in place appropriate policies, structures, etc., including channels of information.

The university rewards system, in terms of promotion, salaries, etc. should reflect the priorities assigned to the various activities in which staff are permitted to engage. As discussed above, that is rarely the case at present, but this problem is being addressed to some extent. If the institution wishes to encourage a pattern of activity, it must emphasise that rewards will go to staff on the basis of their conformity with the pattern. This may mean several alternative routes to success, or perhaps more often a points system based on participation by staff in several activities to the approved extent.

Managing the interface

Cultural differences dictate that the most effective relationships are built up over a period of time. This allows the individuals at the interface to develop a good understanding of the needs and possibilities on both sides. Now it is usual for both universities and companies to have full-time, experienced staff assigned to this role. They will often have worked both in industry and academia.

Where contract research is proposed, it is important for the academic scientist to study the company's R&D problems in depth. The company may not be aware of how the academic can be of best use to it. It may try to spell out the path to be followed too closely, rather than explaining the nature of the problem to be solved. This fails to recognise that the basic researcher's strength is in complex problem-solving. A very different solution to the problem might be more effective than the route considered by the company.

Integrating externally generated technology

It is not enough that the individuals at the interface should communicate with one another. They must be able to communicate effectively with their own side. Particularly on the company side, they must have sufficient standing within their own organisation to introduce new ideas and technologies, sometimes in conflict with some internal interests. It is usually important to keep the people in the large company who will eventually take it in-house well informed about the developing project, and to choose the moment carefully for transferring it into the large company. These points are emphasised by company management with long experience of working at this interface.

THE STRATEGIC QUESTIONS

As initially noted, decisions about the functions to be externalised, about the development of an effective interface, and about a coherent policy for maintaining the core in-house expertise must be fully integrated within the company's long-term strategic plan.

It is important for companies to assess their own needs with great care. After reviewing the situation thoroughly, they should consider the range of options available to them, bearing in mind the practical problems of academic liaison outlined above. Only after this audit has been completed will it be possible to decide whether academic liaison should join the other components of the company's R&D portfolio in the interests of an optimal balancing of risk.

THE WIDER CONTEXT

From the perspective of society as a whole, one might ask whether direct relationships between universities and companies (conducted as suggested above) are the best way to use scarce resources of academic expertise. This is still a matter for debate. Where it is an important source of new technology for local industry, there is a strong case (Mansfield 1991). Where the net beneficiaries over the country as a whole are foreign companies, it is difficult to sustain the argument.

There are only two ways in which one can politically justify this latter situation. First, where the example of successful industrial liaison between local universities and foreign companies leads indigenous companies to exploit these resources more effectively. Second, where local entrepreneurs can interest foreign corporate venturers in backing local technology developments within local new companies which retain their independence. In this case, there is the possibility of substantial returns on the public investment. The probability of either of these outcomes is dependent on other factors within the business environment.

In the next chapter the environment for innovation of the British entrepreneur developing university-derived technology is compared with the parallel situation in the USA. The extent to which it is possible to generalise between the two, and between different points in time, is also examined.

Chapter 8

The environment for innovation in the UK and the USA

How interesting to companies are the novel ideas and technologies emerging from universities? Are they of genuine practical interest to firms planning market-driven product developments? Or are they too remote from the marketplace for consideration by organisations for whom rates of return on investment must be a primary consideration?

In this chapter the UK and US inventive records are compared, and also the main aspects of the US and UK financial, scientific and business environments which influence success at the earlier stages of development of university-derived invention. These records contain a number of rather surprising figures which merit scrutiny.

Both the USA and the UK offer abundant practical possibilities for companies wishing to access university-derived technology. In order to assess their potential, the differing contexts must be taken into account. A close look at the available figures about invention in general and also the portion which is university based puts the UK in an extremely favourable light. In innovation, however, the picture is different.

The three main players in the innovative process – inventors, independent investors and corporate sponsors – are examined, comparing business and market structures. Communication and reward systems affecting the three groups in the two countries are also briefly compared.

INNOVATION

Innovation, the process by which novel or improved products and processes are brought to 'a useful state' (von Hippel 1988), is widely regarded as crucially important to economic progress (Kendrick and Vaccara 1980). Governments are generally anxious to encourage their industries to increase their innovativeness. Considerable efforts are devoted to trying to understand how to create the conditions that foster it effectively.

Definitive solutions have not emerged. However, there is a degree of consensus about some of the factors: it is generally reckoned that a strong flow of inventions, i.e. novel ideas for useful and commercial products and processes, is important. The flow need not be indigenous. The Japanese ability to innovate, on the basis of inventions made elsewhere, has underlined this fact. It has also highlighted the point that the main economic rewards are achieved by the countries whose companies are able to carry innovation through to the marketplace.

Countries that register a relatively high rate of invention are not always equally successful in innovation. Polyester fibre and jet passenger aircraft were both invented in Britain, but British industry has not been the main beneficiary.

Facilitating innovation

With the growth of interest in innovation has come a concern to locate the sources of major inventions, and to identify the factors which assist or block their development towards usefulness.

Technological innovation has been demonstrated to arise from several sources (von Hippel 1988). However, studies suggest that university-derived invention has been a particularly important source of innovation in western industry in this century (Tornatzky *et al.* 1983; Mansfield 1991). This has coincided with increasing awareness on the part of governments of the important role played by institutional scientists in assisting the development of their ideas. One result has been widespread governmental efforts to make university-based invention more accessible for exploitation. In recent years there has been a steady stream of initiatives designed to encourage and reward institutions and scientists for co-operating in exploitation of new technology (see Chapters 2–6).

The results have been generally encouraging, but a variety of problems have been experienced, some general, some reflecting national differences in business and academic cultures.

THE CREATION OF TRANSFERABLE INTELLECTUAL PROPERTY

The seventeenth-century English parliament recognised that it was important for intellectual property to be legally protectable and transferable, like any other piece of property, in order to encourage investment in its commercialisation. Patents and several other types of intellectual property were given a legal status similar to other possessions, although for a finite period of time. This has incidentally created a public record of invention which can be used to track the generators and exploiters of invention.

The limitations to the use of patents and patent application rates as measures of inventiveness have been pointed out (Schankerman and Pakes 1985; Mansfield 1986). Practical problems of interpretation include differences between companies in patenting policies which do not appear to be related to rate of invention. Differing rates of patenting in different countries due to substantial differences in the laws and costs of patenting also create comparison difficulties. There is also the problem that major inventions cannot be distinguished from small, incremental inventions using these data alone.

However, several studies have shown that patent counts can be used effectively as a measure of national R&D productivity (Griliches 1984; Griliches et al. 1986; Scherer 1983; Scherer 1984). By looking at such measures as external patenting and internal patenting data from several countries, usable information can be gleaned. This reveals the rate of generation of inventions regarded by their inventors as worth protecting. In addition, looking at the rate of patenting of, for instance, Japanese and British inventions in the USA, corrects for the legal and cost differences of patenting locally, giving a more accurate way of comparing national performance.

The record of invention

Patent application rates declined in both the USA and the UK in the period 1970–83, but there has been an upturn since then (Cabinet Office 1990). Patents granted on university-derived technology with high income-generating potential have also shown an increase in the years 1988–90 inclusive (BTG 1989).

An OECD report published in 1988 (Englander et al. 1988) showed the UK in 1983 ahead of the US in patent applications, patent grants and external patent applications per scientist or engineer. The UK was also ahead of Japan in external patent applications, though behind France, Germany and Italy. In terms of patents per unit expenditure on R&D, the rate of patent grants and of external patent applications was much higher for the UK than for any other country.

This means that in terms of inventions regarded by their inventors as worth patenting, the UK showed far higher productivity per unit of expenditure than any other country in 1983, although the rate per scientist was lower in the UK than the other major European countries. It was much higher than the corresponding US rate. In number of patents per head of population, the UK was ahead of all countries except Germany and Japan. In the period 1984-8, the rate increased everywhere, and France marginally overtook the UK in terms of US patents granted per head of population (Cabinet Office 1990).

These data portray the UK as generating perceived, commercial ideas at a high rate, especially when compared with the USA. They also reveal that the UK has a much greater return on R&D expenditure in terms of patenting activity compared with its major competitors. Thus it is unlikely that the extensively discussed failure of UK innovation (IAB 1990; Pavitt and Soete 1980) is due to a lack of inventions. Nor is there a failure to recognise the commerciality of the novel ideas. This is indicated by the decision to patent them.

International interest in UK invention

There is another indicator of the high quality of the technology invented in the UK: many British inventions are licensed overseas, rather than being developed by British companies. The USA spent over $491m on licensing UK technology in 1990 – more than it spent on buying technology from any other country (Moffat 1991).

British companies received £615m in royalties from abroad in 1983, and paid £482m in royalties to non-UK organisations for technology licences, a substantial net outflow of technology (Grubb 1986). There was a net outflow of technology in every year between 1979 and 1985. In 1986 and 1987 this was reversed (OECD 1990). No more recent figures are available yet as to whether the trend has definitely changed.

There is more extensive information on the licensing of the inventions regarded as most significant for major new technological developments, i.e. those generated in basic research laboratories in universities and government-funded research institutes (BTG 1989). The British Technology Group (BTG) had until 1985 the first option to patent technology developed with public finance, including the university sector. Since there is a lag between patenting and selling developed products, and since much university technology is still patented by the BTG, its reports to date still include virtually all UK university-derived technology licensing. Its 1990 Annual Report showed a decline in royalty income from UK companies and a steep increase in overseas income through the period 1988–90.

The record of university-based invention

The UK's record of university- and research institute-based invention is outstanding by any measurable criteria. UK and US sources show that in each of the last few years, total royalties paid for licensing UK university- and research institute-derived inventions exceeded the absolute amounts paid for licensing US university- and federal research institute-derived inventions (Harvey 1990; Nelsen 1988b; BTG 1989; BTG 1990). For the year ending March 1990, the BTG's royalty income was $47m and the US university and research institute combined royalty income amounted to $45m.

In the case of the UK, the true total is actually higher than that shown by the BTG, since some university inventions are owned directly by the institutions, whose royalty income is therefore not registered in the BTG's accounts. (BTG's accounts include only royalty income from public sector inventions which it has chosen to exploit.) In addition, UK universities rarely retain IPR in inventions sponsored by companies. Consequently they receive no income in these cases, although they have generated new technology which has been effectively exploited.

These figures suggest that while little of the income generated actually finds its way back to the inventors, university-based invention in the UK is generating greater returns than in the USA. This is in spite of the much greater population and research investment in the USA.

THE INNOVATIVE RECORD

In spite of the good record in invention, the UK's innovative performance has been progressively falling behind that of its international competitors (Pavitt and Soete 1980; IAB 1990). It is therefore necessary to look at the post-invention stages of the commercialisation process to locate the causes for Britain's relatively poor performance in technological innovation.

There are a variety of possible reasons for the current failure of UK companies to exploit the indigenous abundance of inventions. These include unfavourable factors in the general business environment, lack of co-operation between universities and large companies, negative attitudes towards new company formation, and lack of finance for innovation.

THE IMPORTANCE OF UNIVERSITY-DERIVED INNOVATION

University-derived innovation is increasingly recognised as a major source of new technology both for large companies and for small, new companies.

The role of universities in spawning new, technology-based companies with considerable growth potential was recognised in the 1960s. Stanford University and MIT had spun out a number of companies, exploiting technology invented in the universities. With continuing support from the academic institutions, the new ventures grew rapidly and in their turn spun out more companies. These continued to cluster around the supportive focus of the parent institutions (Saxenian 1983; Dorfman 1983). At the same time, large companies began to set up R&D facilities near to the campuses to facilitate technology transfer. Often the large firms had longstanding, collaborative relationships with these universities. This phenomenon attracted considerable interest around the world, and the critical features of industrial liaison activities at these institutions were closely examined.

The first European attempt to emulate Stanford and MIT in this respect was at Heriot-Watt University in Scotland. The story of the founding of Heriot-Watt Research Park is told in Chapter 6.

In the years since then, other British attempts have been made to build new companies or strengthen established firms with university-derived technology. To date, none has succeeded in generating dynamic organisations on the scale and with the frequency of the original US models.

THE LINKAGES IN THE CHAIN OF INNOVATION

Innovation partnerships

Why are there such discrepancies between the British and American innovation records?

There are three important parties to the early innovation process: inventors, financiers and corporate sponsors/buyers. If the inventor cannot personally finance innovation, he, or his institution must seek external sponsorship. In some cases, a large corporation may be willing to take the invention in-house at this point. This is more likely to be the case if the initial research has been sponsored by a firm with an interest in carrying the invention forward. Where there is no interested corporate sponsor already present, either one must be sought or else independent finance must be obtained to assist in development. This is usually in the form of equity capital for a new company, developing the product/process.

Another alternative which is often employed, particularly in Europe, is to use a technology broker to find a licensee for the invention. In the UK this is frequently the method of choice, usually through the medium of the BTG. This organisation no longer enjoys a monopoly of public sector inventions, but is still used extensively by UK universities. All West European countries have comparable government organisations. There are also a number of private technology brokers operating throughout Europe and the USA.

The academic inventor's conflicting priorities

When the time comes to decide between these possible courses of action, scientists are faced with difficult choices. As discussed in Chapter 7, the scientist is rewarded in the university and the world of science for publishing as much high quality, basic research as possible (Merton 1973; Gaston 1978). Neglecting a scientific career to pursue funding for a start-up company reduces the likelihood of academic rewards. On the other hand, if the scientist is successful in obtaining funding, and the company does well, he or she can expect to be rewarded financially. The attractiveness of this prospect will depend on the projected growth prospects of the company, and on the scientist's share of the equity.

While there is evidence that university scientists in the USA were no more eager than their UK colleagues to become involved with business in the 1970s (Wade 1977; Pajaro 1982), academic attitudes have changed in both countries. There is a fairly wide acceptance of the need to commercialise university-generated inventions (Raub 1981; MORI 1989). The main difference between the current attitudes of scientists in the two countries now appears to be in expectations of reward from involvement with industry: many US scientists have made fortunes through their activities in new companies (Bylinsky 1976). Records of similar experiences in the UK are hard to find (Arthur Young 1988).

Thus, while the US scientist is encouraged by witnessing colleagues' success, the UK scientist sees little encouragement to risk his or her academic prospects by trying to set up a company. It seems probable that this lack of attractive local models is a contributing factor to the lower level of interest in forming new companies to exploit UK university-generated technology (Arthur Young 1988).

However, the fact that UK scientist-inventors patent their ideas at such a high rate, especially relative to US scientists, argues that they are at least as aware of the commercial usefulness of their ideas. Choosing to patent also indicates their desire or that of their institution to exploit them. Their attitudes as revealed in a recent survey (MORI 1989) also appear to be very positive towards exploitation. Thus it is difficult to conclude that the UK innovative failure is a consequence of UK scientists' greater reluctance to be associated with commerce.

Finance for innovation

In spite of the shortage of successful role models, many UK scientists and entrepreneurs do try to exploit their inventions directly. The first hurdle they must negotiate is obtaining financial backing. It is generally admitted that there is a shortage of 'seed' capital, i.e. equity capital for start-ups, in the UK (Murray 1990; Shennan 1990). This has not always been the case. In Britain, early vehicles for pooling venture capital had been developed by the sixteenth century, such as the risk capital partnership which funded Sir Francis Drake's voyage of 1577–80. That particular venture returned a profit of 4,600 per cent, after the Queen had taken her share of the treasure (Heaton 1948). Not all subsequent ventures have been so lucrative, but the current famine of start-up finance in the UK is still somewhat surprising, in the light of the generally encouraging experience of the past.

One explanation which has been suggested is that the high contemporary UK cost of capital makes it harder to achieve an adequate return on very risky investments (James 1990). This, incidentally, is also often blamed for the reluctance of large UK companies to commit resources to innovation.

Cost of capital studies which adjust extensively for different tax structures, inflation rates, accounting practice, etc. show that the average cost of capital in the UK and USA was significantly higher than in Japan or West Germany over the period 1977–88 (McCauley and Zimmer 1989; SCST 1991). After allowing for these adjustments, between mid-1977 and mid-1980 the UK cost was higher than the US cost, while between mid-1981 to 1988 it ranged between 0–2 per cent lower than the US, usually about 1 per cent less at about 5 per cent real after tax cost (Plender 1990). Since the differences of tax structures and other variables are set in place by governments with the specific aim of creating a more favourable environment than those of competitors, then the effective, real-world investment costs for companies are probably much more favourable in Japan and Germany than the adjusted figures suggest. Another study puts the cost of capital for a UK R&D project 70 per cent higher than in Germany and three times the cost of the same project in Japan (McCauley and Zimmer 1989). The much higher price/earnings ratio of the Japanese stock market certainly implies that this is a more meaningful estimate.

With or without adjustment, these figures could certainly be cited to explain the relatively high German and Japanese levels of investment in corporate innovation. They are not a sufficient explanation of why the UK lags behind the USA in exploiting university-based invention in start-up companies. There is a growing body of evidence to support the claim that there is an absolute shortage of seed finance for high technology companies in the UK – that there is insufficient capital available at any price.

Absence of start-up finance

Whatever the reasons, seed capital is not an area which is growing in attractiveness to UK venture capitalists. According to the British Venture Capital Association (BVCA), the percentage of venture capital that went into start-ups declined to 6 per cent in 1989 compared with 8 per cent in 1987. The actual number of start-up financings fell from 191 in 1987 to 177 in 1989. The average amount invested in a 1989 'start-up' was £486,000 (BVCA 1990).

Whether these are really start-ups is a moot point. When companies require smaller amounts of initial capital, they have great difficulty finding any organisation willing to consider smaller-scale projects. Of the 127 organisations offering venture finance which are listed in the BVCA 1990 directory, only thirty-three claim to be willing to consider placing less than £100,000. An additional thirty-eight will consider investments of less than £250,000. Virtually all of them state that their preferred investment is much higher than their minimum.

A report by Bain & Company (1990) gave a figure of 0.1 per cent of venture funds invested in seed capital in the UK, compared with 0.2 per cent in France and 2 per cent in the USA.

There is also the problem of lack of investor interest in technology-related ventures. In 1989 the single most important sector for UK venture investment was consumer-related businesses, i.e. leisure, retailing, etc. In that year 25 per cent of all companies financed and 45 per cent of the total amount invested were in this category (BVCA 1990). In fact, much of this investment was in buy-out activity in the retailing business. In 1990, investment in technology was down to 12 per cent from 16 per cent in 1987 (Bain & Company 1990). US venture investment in technology was of the order of 65 per cent in the same period (ibid.). These figures confirm the reluctance of British venture capitalists to back more than a handful of technology-related start-ups.

Small amounts of equity finance are available through special seed funds set up by public/private sector syndicates, such as the £2.5m venture fund set up by the National Westminster Bank and St John's College, Cambridge, in 1990 (*Financial Times* 1990). Several universities, often in association with their science parks, have small funds of this sort. The sums involved are still totally insufficient to meet the demands.

Financing US start-ups

How does the US compare? Contrary to the impression usually given by commentators, US venture capital companies do not appear to be a major source of finance for start-ups, either. A recent survey carried out by the US government's provider of finance and advice to small firms, the Small Business Administration (SBA) revealed that private investors or 'business angels' are the largest source of external equity capital for early-stage businesses in the USA. They invest at least two or three times the $4bn invested annually by US venture capital companies (Gaston and Bell 1990). They invest in very small firms, making on average two investments within 3 years, usually along with two other investors. On average, the investing group make about $150,000 and their personal expertise available to an investee company, and hold their invest-ment for 5.1 years. They are generally satisfied with the performance of their investments and expect to make others.

An interesting point noted in this report is that the US market for new ventures is made up of a very large number of small, local markets in which information is passed on informally and transac-tions are mainly conducted in private. This contrasts with the UK technology venture capital market, where specialist firms are heavily concentrated in London.

The SBA survey did not clarify the matter of the 'angels' ' exit from their investments. However, whether the investee companies' first expansion was funded by earnings, formal venture capital or other external sources, the situation a little further down the road is much more favourable in the USA than in the UK.

Development capital in the USA

The largest over-the-counter market in the USA, NASDAQ, with more than 4,000 companies listed, offers the possibility of a genuine equity market with substantial liquidity for small-to-medium com-panies requiring development capital. The level of trading in even quite small companies is active compared with the Unlisted Secur-ities Market (USM) in London (see Tables 8.1 and 8.2). What is more, while the requirements for disclosure are relatively stringent, there is no requirement for forecasts of imminent profitability. The USM, on the other hand, requires predictions of profits within one year as a precondition of listing. This is quite unrealistic for technology-based companies looking for development capital which often require millions of pounds of project finance, but with probably 3–5 years of product development ahead before any revenue is projected (Jack 1990).

The quality of a market is a function of several variables, including the number of market-makers; their willingness to make

Table 8.1   NASDAQ market quality

Company	*m.v.* $m	*s.p.* $	*e.p.s.* $	*Half-yearly vol.* as % of shares out
Hana	13	1.9	n/a	44
Monoclon Anti Inc.	16	4.1	n/a	80
Ribi Imm	24	2.7	n/a	33
Vestar	28	4.3	n/a	16
Biotech Res Labs	28	4.5	n/a	24
Ecogen	29	4.3	n/a	27
Neorx	45	3.0	n/a	41
Mycogen	83	10.1	n/a	7
Invitron	98	6.5	n/a	25
Genzyme	170	14.2	0.08	78
Genetics Inst.	427	30.5	-0.81	114

Notes:
m.v. = market value 1.11.89
s.p. = share price 1.11.89
e.p.s. = earnings per share 1988
n/a = not applicable

Source: Paine Webber

markets continuously; transaction costs; and liquidity. Of these, liquidity is perhaps the most important. In order to gain some idea of the relative liquidity of NASDAQ versus the USM, the following relationship is proposed: the proportion of a company's stock which changes hands over an annualised period of 'normal' trading indicates the level of liquidity of the market for that company.

Trading volumes for eleven publicly quoted, US technology-based companies are given in Table 8.1. The stocks are traded on the largest American OTC market, NASDAQ. The period chosen was November 1989, a relatively recent date and also a period of relatively 'normal' trading, low by the standards of the bull market period of the 1980s, but preceding the unstable period of 1990. It was not a period of high popularity of technology stocks.

Column 5 shows the liquidity of the stock, expressed as follows: average daily volume in November 1989 was multiplied by 240, the approximate number of trading days in a year. This figure (in '000s of shares) was then expressed as a percentage of total shares outstanding. Since the trading volume is calculated as the number of shares sold plus the number bought, this percentage was divided by two, to give an estimated figure for the *percentage of the*

Table 8.2   USM market quality

Company	m.v. £m	s.p. pence	e.p.s. pence	Half-yearly vol. as % shares out
†Maxiprint	2.40	14	n/a	1.49
*Norbain Electron	2.80	30	2.4	10.87
†Ommitech	4.50	25	n/a	2.06
*Plasmec	4.97	108	5.6	0.07
*CPU Computing	6.96	40	2.4	0.03
†Plastiseal	8.41	107	9.6	15.04
*Microvitec	8.57	31.5	n/a	4.89
Security Archiv	9.08	145	13.0	3.43
†Micrelec	16.12	152	11.8	2.64
*CML Micro	29.41	171	16.7	1.05
*ML Labs	112.75	451	n/a	12.4

Notes:
m.v. = market value 1.11.89
s.p. = share price 1.11.89
e.p.s. = earnings per share 1988
n/a = not applicable

*Technology Stock
†Industrial Stock
Source: Datastream

company which changes hands in a normal year. No allowance for intramarket trading is made. The market value and share price on 1 November 1989 and earnings per share for 1988 (where available) are also tabulated.

In order to compare the liquidity of NASDAQ with that of the UK Unlisted Securities Market, data for eleven USM companies is given in Table 8.2 in a similar format to that of the NASDAQ companies given in Table 8.1. Six of the companies are technology stocks. For an explanation of the calculations performed, see previous figure.

The Datastream figures for volume are calculated as follows: customers plus 1/2 principals. This is to correct for intramarket trading. This is only an estimate and may give rise to variable inaccuracies. The parallel figures for NASDAQ have no such correction, but no data are available about the extent of intramarket trading. Thus volume figures for both markets are only approximate. However, the differences in levels of trading are so great that this should not significantly affect the conclusions.

Since there are currently only forty technology stocks quoted on the USM, of which at most two could be classified as biotechnology stocks, it is not possible to construct a sample which is directly comparable with the group of NASDAQ stocks. Consequently the sample here has been selected from both technology and industrial stocks. Eleven companies of low-to-medium market valuation, roughly comparable to the NASDAQ sample's range, are included. The trading volumes of the USM stocks are markedly lower than those of the NASDAQ stocks, on average. On both markets there is considerable variation in trading volume, unrelated to market valuation. Some of this may be due to the irregularity of trading of individual stocks – often smaller stocks are not traded for some time, then there is heavy trading reflecting good news or some other event. However, there is virtually no overlap between the range of volumes on NASDAQ and the much lower average volumes on the USM. Eight of the USM companies showed less than 5 per cent of the company traded annually. Only one NASDAQ company fell below 16 per cent.

The absolute market valuations of the NASDAQ companies are slightly higher on average than those of the USM companies. Earnings per share for the NASDAQ companies were mostly negative, and none was substantial, while four out of the six technology stocks on the USM had positive earnings per share. Thus the greater level of investor interest in NASDAQ is not a reflection of higher current earnings.

Market information

NASDAQ offers other attractions: sponsorship of small companies by reputable market-makers with substantial resources and a strong client base. Stockbrokers dealing in smaller companies' stock publicise their clients, creating a very extensive body of information about the small technology company sector, new products, both potential and on the market, joint ventures, etc. This generates a high level of investor knowledge and interest in early-stage ventures, an important feature for the efficient working of the market. The standing of the sponsors also lends credibility to the companies they publicise.

The need for a market

The existence of an active public market for small companies still in the development stage is very likely to affect willingness of venture capitalists to invest in the earlier stages. The life of a venture fund is usually finite, 7–12 years on average (Hector 1985). Fund managers make new investments through the early years, and they must be able to realise most of their investment and distribute the returns to investors by the end of the fixed period. The alternatives are to 'roll over' a portion of the holdings into a new fund, or to distribute the illiquid stocks, neither of which is very desirable from the standpoints of either the fund managers or the investors.

In the absence of an effective public market, the task of finding buyers for the investee companies is onerous. Usually, in the case of technology-based companies, a 'trade sale' to a large company is the only alternative exit route (Abingworth 1989). A few non-US companies have actually chosen to go public on NASDAQ first, as the best means of accessing the equity markets, for example, Biogen N.V. (Netherlands Antilles, but basically a joint European/American venture), Elan (Irish) and Huntingdon International (UK). This is obviously much more difficult for a non-US company, in a market where most investors are not familiar with the investee company's operating environment.

Why has Britain's USM failed where NASDAQ has been such a success? There are probably a number of contributory factors. Size is the most obvious. The number and combined financial mass of the companies within individual sectors quoted on NASDAQ justifies substantial commitment to them by brokers. Then there is the UK's reliance on institutional shareholders who can only buy 'large stocks', given the size of the pools of funds – only 17 per cent of total shareholdings are in the hands of individual investors, compared with 66 per cent in the USA (IAB 1990). The UK habit of saving through pension funds and insurance companies where investment decisions are made by professional fund managers may well be a factor in the low popularity of the USM compared with the American OTC markets.

Corporate sponsorship

The other source of support to which the inventor can look is the corporate sponsor. Large, technology-based companies are important sponsors of university-based or small company innovation. They are frequently not only a source of finance and development expertise but also the ultimate purchasers of the new product or process technology (Abingworth 1989). Their interest in the development of inventions stems from self-interest. They can have access to new technology without the necessity, at least in the short term, of making as great a commitment to it as would be required by investment in full, in-house development of comparable technology.

Superficially, this would appear to be the ideal strategy for companies who wish to minimise their immediate R&D expenditure. Thus it ought to appeal to the many companies in Britain who are cutting back on R&D (Freeman 1990; IAB 1990). In fact, UK companies seem to be trailing behind the field in this activity (Freeman 1990; Bain 1990). US, Japanese and Swiss companies are among the prominent international operators and Germans continue their longstanding (Beer 1959) practice of very close interaction between German academics and companies.

Relatively few UK companies are making a high-profile commitment to corporate sponsorship. BP plc (BP 1989) and ICI plc (*Northern Echo* 1990) are among the exceptions. However, it is more common to see announcements of non-UK companies' corporate investments in small, UK, high technology companies, e.g. Monsanto's investment in Oxford Glycosystems Ltd (Clarke 1989b), and Japan Tobacco and JafCo's investment in British Biotechnology Ltd (British Biotechnology Group 1990).

This apparent lack of interest among large UK companies in corporate venturing is paralleled by the relatively low level of UK company involvement at the invention stage within UK universities: at Oxford University, 80 per cent of corporate sponsorship of research is by non-UK companies (Clark 1989a). This may in turn be a function of the fact that UK companies on the whole have a limited and declining commitment to any sort of R&D: twenty companies account for over 60 per cent of R&D in the UK (Freeman 1990). The small number of companies with a serious commitment to innovation restricts the absolute number of potential sponsors, and also the range of technologies in which they have an interest in encouraging developments.

R&D MANAGEMENT IN LARGE EC COMPANIES

The roots of the problem may lie in the widely deplored and unsatisfactory approach to R&D management commonly encountered in many EC countries. A survey of seventy of its European member companies carried out by the European Industrial Research Managers' Association (EIRMA) showed that, while senior R&D management contributed proposals to corporate decision-making in 58 per cent of the organisations, in only 9 per cent did they play any role in actual decision-making. In 20 per cent of organisations, mainly the larger companies, the R&D strategy document was not communicated back to those contributing proposals to it (EIRMA 1986).

The same study showed that more than 80 per cent of the companies considered the ratio of internal/external R&D in planning R&D strategy. However, without full involvement of R&D management, it is unlikely that this could translate itself into a productive programme of corporate venturing.

Unfortunately, this study does not break the figures down by nation. Evidence from other studies indicates that in the UK, R&D planning is rarely integrated into strategic planning. An evaluation of the ESPRIT programme, an EC-funded collaborative R&D programme in information technology involving small and large companies and university researchers, commented that links between R&D and production divisions of large UK companies in the programme were weak (Hare *et al.* 1989). This is not a new problem. Cultural barriers between the production and marketing divisions of companies have long created communication difficulties, especially in larger companies (Freeman 1986; Burns and Stalker 1961).

The extent to which technology strategy is integrated into the mainstream of corporate planning is likely to affect the speed and effectiveness of a company's response to new technological opportunities and threats. This, in turn, is likely to be affected by the importance of the role given to technical directors within the company in corporate strategy formulation. Corporate sponsorship by UK companies is thus unlikely to fill the gaps for small innovative companies until its general strategic usefulness for large companies is more widely appreciated and incorporated into the strategic planning function.

CONCLUSION

What useful conclusions can be drawn from this limited comparison of the environments for innovation in the UK and the USA? Several points are clear:

1 Lack of inventiveness is not the problem in the UK. There is no lack of commercial new ideas in Britain. The excellent patent record, which compares very favourably with that of the USA, demonstrates this. The fact that the inventors recognise and wish to exploit the commercial potential is indicated by the decision to patent. This fact also invalidates suggestions that UK scientist-inventors are more averse to association with commerce than their American counterparts. Any doubts about the value of UK inventions are countered by the high rate at which they are licensed abroad.

2 Lack of some types of finance is a problem. There seem to be gaps in the linkages in the innovation process in the UK. American inventors and entrepreneurs can look to a series of well-established sources of finance. These cover their needs from the earliest stage at which small amounts of external support are needed, through later rounds of formal venture capital-sourced mezzanine funding, to public offerings drawing on the abundant liquidity of the large, well-informed OTC markets. The British inventor, on the other hand, suffers a severe lack of early-stage finance, and later on finds it difficult to interest venture funds, partly because they have problems in exiting from cash-hungry technology R&D company investments. Thus lack of seed capital at the start, and of a good OTC market at the end of the innovation process are causing difficulties for new company formation in the UK.

3 There is a shortage of UK corporate sponsors. Most UK companies appear to lack enthusiasm for corporate venturing. This may be due to failure to integrate R&D planning fully into corporate strategy.

4 UK inventors do not have much in the way of role models to show them how to commercialise their inventions. This shortage of convincing local models also means that there is little to entice them with the prospect of rich rewards to compensate for the risks they must take in trying to exploit their inventions. In spite of this, survey data suggest that they are interested in personal involvement in the exploitation of their inventions.

5 In the UK, technology brokers play a significant role in mediating between academic inventors and companies. This allows exploitation, but exports most of the innovation and consequently most of the financial returns.

The lesson from America

This adds up to a discouraging picture for the UK inventor who wishes to play an active role in exploitation.

Continuity of support is essential. Appropriate expertise and finance must be available to underpin all the stages of the innovation process. If gaps yawn at any stage, the initial investment in many useful inventions will be lost because there is no means to carry them to the market. This obvious, but widely ignored fact will remain true in any business environment. No matter how different the paths followed, they must always run unbroken from start to finish.

Moving up the learning curve

Perhaps it is premature to castigate British failure to rival American success in exploiting novel technology. The earliest successes of Silicon Valley and Route 128 were not funded with venture capital, which was attracted to these areas after a great track record of profitability had been established by the first spin-out companies (Saxenian 1983; Dorfman 1983). Since then, American venture capitalists have had a substantial period of time to develop their expertise.

The 'biotechnology revolution' of the late 1970s and 1980s was funded by venture capitalists who had great confidence in the commercialisability of new US technology, thanks to their previous lucrative ventures in microelectronics. Even now, the main providers of US start-up finance are not venture capital companies but the informal local groups of investors described above (Gaston and Bell 1990). This is the category which is conspicuously lacking in the UK, and this may hold the real key to future success.

Conceivably, this role may now be filled by the new local enterprise companies in the UK. Certainly, the provision of relatively small sums of seed capital, along with the input of expertise and real interest of the local business community, should be much more possible within the LEC structure. It is not difficult to envisage ways of raising the funds required, especially if very modest fiscal encouragement were to be offered.

The later-stage problems of lack of information and liquid equity markets for developing companies may be in the process of being resolved. EC-wide efforts to extend and co-ordinate business information sources are improving information flow and accessibility. Moves to link stock markets and harmonise listing rules may be helpful to smaller companies, providing special efforts are made to accommodate their needs. It is not yet possible to predict how the changes will work.

The outlook

There are undoubtedly barriers to innovation in the UK by the start-up company route at present. These could conceivably be reduced by a pragmatic approach, exemplified by the successful American model. The early-stage problems focused on here should be amenable to commonsense solutions. The later-stage problems will possibly be addressed in the developing pan-European framework, providing the current awareness of small companies' problems is maintained.

On the other hand, for the large company looking for new technology, the outlook in the UK is promising. The current changes in the structures supporting university/industry co-operation offer greatly improved possibilities for large companies wishing to exploit the expertise and inventiveness of the universities.

Chapter 9

The track record to date

More innovation in a wider range of technologies is taking place now than in any previous era. One of the most outstanding features of our time is the sheer abundance of new technologies and innovation, and also of novel combinations of technologies creating new possibilities. Another characteristic of current patterns of technological development is that they are often closely intertwined with contemporary advances in basic science (Stankiewicz 1986; Mansfield 1991). This is one of the major factors driving the trend towards closer involvement between company and university scientists. The universities are seen to be an important source, not just of the ultimate intellectual roots of new technologies, but of commercially valuable skills and patentable inventions.

In the UK and the USA there is considerable public anxiety that rates of innovation are not keeping pace with those of economic competitors. This, in turn, has led to the growth of interest in the role of university-based research in innovation. Until recently, the British and American universities' economic role had been seen primarily in terms of the provision of trained manpower. Their structure, reward systems and relationships with government were not designed to optimise the exploitation of their research. Now there is a widespread perception of the need to improve the quality and quantity of interaction between universities and companies. This is focusing the efforts of governments, of companies, and of the academic institutions themselves. A consensus is evolving about ways to optimise these interactions from the points of view of all of the participants. The potential for conflict between organisations with different objectives and cultures is being contained by creating new structures and policies. These are being put in place to permit the traditional activities of universities to be pursued in parallel with collaborative activities with companies.

Unfortunately, the most important outcomes of the current arrangements will be impossible to assess until it is too late to change the support systems. The more significant effects aimed for are general improvements in company and industry performance, and increased innovativeness. These are outcomes with complex causes which are difficult to disentangle. They cannot be measured meaningfully over short periods of time. It is also impossible to separate out completely the relative contribution of each of the environmental factors influencing these changes.

The indicative measures which have been discussed in previous chapters are the easiest to isolate. The number of campus-derived patents and the level of licensing income, the increasing level of commercial contract-funding of campus research, the joint research laboratories which have attracted increasing private sector support, these are easy to count. So are the number of products and processes, especially in high technology industries, which companies claim have had essential campus inputs (Mansfield 1991). The frequent announcements in the financial press of domestic and overseas companies setting up research laboratories on campus, and their joint ventures with campus-derived companies, are also indicators of the importance the international business community sets on campus skills and technology.

Some of these might be measures of the success universities have had in promoting themselves to companies, rather than a true reflection of the value companies are receiving for their investment. However, the more substantial commitments have mainly been made after at least a few years of fruitful interaction on a more modest scale. They are not high-risk ventures. They have been constructed on a solid base of mutual understanding. Looking at the results of longer-standing experiments in industrial liaison, it seems likely that at least some will prosper and generate significant successes. Given the past experience they are built on, they should be less prone to failure than earlier experiments. Companies are now in a better position to optimise their industrial liaison, using the accumulated knowledge gleaned from analysis of past efforts.

In spite of these very positive signs, improvement of relations in the USA and the UK between campus and company has still a long way to go. Companies complain of the difficulties in finding the ideas and the people they need to help them. Both sides complain of disappointments and misunderstandings. Where university

scientists and industry are unable to develop successful relationships, the suggestion is that this is owing to either a failure in
information flows or to excessive transaction costs (Stankiewicz
1986).

On the other hand, the growing experience of campus/company
collaborations has created workable management and legal
formulas for initiating and maintaining them, and joint organisational structures which offer ways around the barriers. There is
growing recognition of the need for more efficient information
transfer, and for subsidies during the initial stages until the pattern
of mutually profitable interaction has been established. Policies and
practice are not yet perfected, but they are now reasonably effective
in many organisations, and they are steadily improving.

CONTINUING PROBLEMS FROM THE UNIVERSITIES' PERSPECTIVE

Differing priorities

There will continue to be conflicts about priorities – technology
seeks concrete results versus the universal laws sought by science
(Ben-David 1971). But scientists also develop technologies to
produce concrete results in the pursuit of universal laws, and these
technologies are often commercially valuable. The techniques of
genetic engineering are an outstanding example of this. Thus
scientists will always have plenty of ammunition with which to
defend themselves against the charge that basic research is 'useless'.

Disciplinary divisions of universities

The disciplinary divisions within the universities create difficulties
for interaction with industry, whose own imperatives often cross
disciplinary boundaries. This is being tackled in many institutions
in special interdisciplinary centres, often with industrial partners.
The problems will not be abolished, but hopefully they will be
managed in an increasingly effective manner in this context.

Cultural incompatibility

There are still incompatibilities between the culture of the company
and that of the university. Secrecy versus free dissemination is a

major stumbling block. Academic scientists' career progress depends on their reputations: 'Yes, Virginia, scientists do love recognition, but only since Pythagoras' (Lederman 1969). Control of IPR and organisational incompatibility may continue to be potential causes of conflict, but as norms are progressively established, this will diminish in importance.

PROBLEMS FROM THE COMPANY PERSPECTIVE

Controlling time horizons

New products must be brought to market on schedule. University scientists have other priorities. As mutual experience is developed, scientists acquire a better understanding of the need to respect company objectives in order to retain the advantages of industrial sponsorship. Companies report considerable differences here, not only between individual laboratories, but also between universities. Some are much more responsive than others.

This is not a problem that is likely to disappear altogether. It will necessarily affect the emphasis companies will choose to put on the different types of interaction with the campus. Collaborative activities should, after all, be entered into with the most appropriate partner. Product development is probably not a suitable activity for a university laboratory under most circumstances. Perhaps when a project reaches this stage, the company should take it in-house, or the university should form a company around it, for exploitation.

On the other hand, joint research activities with both basic and applied interest, where company scientists are benefiting from the interaction with campus expertise, are more in tune with campus values and will probably prove rewarding. Where the characteristics of the whole industrial network as it affects a particular project are well understood, the organisations within the network will be more likely to form relationships that will endure and yield satisfactory outcomes.

The interface between company and institution

This interface, and the procedures for bringing a project in-house, must be carefully planned. Timing is crucial. If the transition is made either too early or too late, the accumulated experience of practitioners predicts it is unlikely to be successful. A continuing consultancy arrangement with the inventor may help. Again, the quality of the relationship is important, and investment in this over time will improve the communication which must take place for a successful transition into the company. Where the individuals who must work together to take the project in-house have developed a good relationship, this is more likely to occur.

OPTIMISING THE RELATIONSHIP

The rules for optimising relationships between the company and the university are basically the same as for any good client/supplier relationship. However, because of the unusually great difference in cultures, the situation is more demanding on both sides than more conventional sourcing relationships.

Collaboration between industry and academia will always require some tolerance of ambiguity and a willingness to be adaptable. Where possible, the rules of the relationship should be clarified at the outset. They must also be modifiable, by mutual consent, as circumstances change, but at any one time the operating framework should be well understood by all parties. This must not be so rigid that it prevents the individuals concerned from actually carrying out the work of the collaboration and achieving the required results. Clear objectives and regular monitoring are essential, but not precise prescription down to the last detail. Each collaboration should have some 'self-designing' power over its own process (Benassi 1991).

These are not problems which are peculiar to the academic/corporate marriage. Both university and company personnel are obliged to operate in other contexts where similar difficulties arise. Academics within their institutions are required to perform activities previously thought to be the province of businessmen – writing business plans, account-keeping, and so on. At the same time, management strategists are advocating that companies should adopt management styles and structures which have more in common with the looser, less hierarchical structure of the university, and which often involve greater emphasis on networks and collaborative groupings. By increasing the common ground of experience between academics and managers, these trends could reduce the potential for friction between the two types of organisations.

THE TRIUMPH OF THE MARKET

Perhaps more than anything else, the pervasive use of marketing concepts in the language used by all working groups is creating a lingua franca. The existence of a common conceptual language, no matter how limited, smoothes communication between occupational cultures. It offers a point of intersection from which to explore the other organisation's needs and objectives.

Academics can now present their knowledge and expertise as products and services which are available, at a price, to the interested company. It was not always acceptable for them to perceive themselves and their work in this light. Companies, in turn, offer rewards in terms of improved research funding and facilities on campus, personal payment for services rendered, and other acceptable currency. This has created a greater comprehension of the area in which they can interact, where there can be mutual interests. It has also increased awareness of the areas which lie outside this common zone, which are important to one or other of the groups, but not to both.

IS THE UNIVERSITY RESOURCE FULLY EXPLOITED?

With so much activity already in the realm of university/industry technology transfer, it might be questioned whether there is any room for additional industrial participants. This does not appear to be a major constraint. Studies carried out on several occasions at MIT suggest that there is a vast reservoir of unexploited technology with recognised commercial potential. In 1969, at least half the technical ideas of commercial interest at MIT were simply not pursued (Peters and Roberts 1969), and more recent evidence suggests a continuing overabundance. The BTG's MORI report (1989) suggests that the situation is similar in the UK.

All the indicators suggest that the importance of company/campus interactions will continue to grow for the foreseeable future. Relationships will become more complex as the mutual benefits are realised. Paradoxically, both the internationalisation of links and the intensity of local interaction are likely to increase. The need for companies to locate very specific, rare expertise will continue to encourage international collaboration. At the same time, the difficulties of managing the relationship will make it desirable for companies to have a local presence, in order to access rare university skills. For all, including smaller companies, it will be desirable, and perhaps increasingly easy, to use the facilities of institutions nearby.

THE PUBLIC POLICY PROBLEM

One problem which has not been explored in detail here is that of the foreign company accessing scarce academic resources. This is a contentious area, particularly in the USA where Japanese ability to commercialise technology invented at great cost to the American taxpayer has become a heated political issue. However, American, British and other multinationals are also significant users of university-based expertise in other countries. There is also some likelihood that many individual laboratories, which currently enjoy foreign support for their very specialised projects, would have difficulty replacing their sponsors with domestic patrons.

The most positive solution would be for new technology to be more frequently exploited within spin-out companies. Through these, there is a far greater probability of national economies obtaining an adequate return on their investment in training and basic research. At least in the UK, this is not likely to happen unless the problems of the environment for innovation are addressed more effectively.

This will need serious consideration at the level of the Commission of the European Communities, as well as at national level, if the current situation is not to deteriorate. The trend at present is towards structures that favour large companies, although there are some possibilities which could be effectively exploited by small companies, particularly high technology companies. EC-wide standards may be costly to meet, but they open up larger markets to small companies, as does the freer flow of information within the community (Bower 1991b).

Whatever the outcome of these debates, it is unlikely to have a significant effect on companies' and universities' mutual desire for interaction. In spite of the inherent problems, companies and universities in a competitive world are discovering that their need for each other is too great to be denied.

Appendix
Information sources for European technology

ACCESSING UK TECHNOLOGY

There are several main information sources for accessing UK public sector technology:

Longman Cartermill maintains the only extensive database of UK academic expertise and innovation (BEST), available on compact disk or online. It also publishes a periodical, *Innovation*, which lists new ideas and inventions looking for sponsors. The European Community database PROTEAS, which is developing coverage of European healthcare and biotechnology innovation, is also available from Longman. CABI Abstracts, online, CD-ROM, or hard copy, covers international agbiotech research with good coverage of the UK and Europe. These sources are inevitably incomplete, but they are improving their coverage constantly.

Direct contact with institutions and their scientists is one way of obtaining more information. Most universities have Directors of Industrial Liaison to interface between the institution and companies or other external groups. They publish data about their institutions' technological expertise, services, inventions and licensing policy. Their professional association, UDIL, publishes a free booklet with contact addresses for all the universities in the UK and Eire, together with listings on their areas of expertise.

Hobsons publishes a directory with similar information to the UDIL Directory, but with more detail and covering a wider range of educational institutions.

There are also intermediaries who can help. Two technology brokers specialise in licensing intellectual property generated in university and other government-funded laboratories: the British Technology Group and 3I Research Exploitation Ltd. They take ownership of the IPR and carry detailed listings of inventions available for licensing. Their coverage is very incomplete since they select the inventions which they expect to generate high licensing income. In addition, universities do not always choose to use their services. However, they are easy to access and they are highly experienced in patenting and licensing. BTG also has a US office which handles both British IPR and, as of 1991, it is trying to build up an American university clientele.

The MRC has a central office handling industrial liaison. The AFRC leaves responsibility for commercial exploitation with its institutes, but it will provide information about their addresses and research coverage.

The UK government Department of Trade and Industry is currently (1991) sponsoring more effective links between industry and academia. It has set up a series of regional technology centres which have information about their local higher education institutions and the expertise they can offer. There are also a number of grant-aided schemes available to subsidise industry/academic links. Information is available from the DTI.

EUROPEAN COMMUNITY

Information about the research activities supported by the Community can be accessed through CORDIS, an information service of the EC. Its databases contain information on all Community-sponsored programmes, project descriptions from all programmes, and abstracts of reports and publications. It can be accessed direct through the ECHO host in Luxembourg. It is currently free of charge. Further information available from Longman Cartermill.

The European Association for the Transfer of Technologies, Innovation and Industrial Information (TII) is an association of technology suppliers and brokers. Its aim is to stimulate innovation and promote technology transfer in the EC. Suppliers include R&D organisations, technology consultants, universities, industrial research associations, manufacturing and service firms. It publishes a directory of its members' names and addresses classified by country, activity, clientele and specialisations. It also offers a range of ancillary services to its members, including a newsletter information service, conference organising service, etc.

Addresses

To obtain the free UDIL Directory:	Bureau of Industrial Liaison, University of Surrey, Guildford GU2 5XH	tel: 0483 571281 fax: 0483 300803
'Higher Education Resources for Industry' £12.50+pp	Hobsons Publishing plc, Bateman St, Cambridge CB2 1LZ	tel: 0223 354551
'Innovation' BEST database PROTEAS database	Director of Marketing, Longman Cartermill Ltd, Technology Centre, St Andrews, Fife KY16 9EA Scotland	tel: 0334 77660 fax: 0334 77180
CORDIS	Ailie Menzies also at Longman Cartermill Ltd	
CAB Abstracts	CAB International, Headquarters, Wallingford, Oxon OX10 8DE or	tel: 0491 32111 fax: 0491 33508
	CAB International, North America, 845 North Park Ave., Tucson, Arizona 85719	tel: 800/528-4841 602/621-7897 fax: 602/621-3816
Technology Brokers	British Technology Group, 101 Newington Causeway, London SE1 6BU	tel: 071 403 6666 fax: 071 403 7586
	3I Research Exploitation Ltd, The Gate House, 2 Park St, Windsor, Berkshire SL4 1LU	tel: 0753 840694 fax: 0753 859776
UK Government Research Institutes	Industrial Liaison Group, Medical Research Council, 20 Park Crescent, London W1N 4AL	tel: 071 636 5422 fax: 071 436 6179
	Agriculture and Food Research Council, Commercial Section,	tel: 0793 514242

	Wiltshire Court, Farnsby St, Swindon SN1 5AT	
Department of Trade and Industry (DTI)	151 Buckingham Palace Road, London SW1W 9SS	tel: 071 215 5000 fax: 071 215 2909
TII	3 rue des Capucins, L-1313 Luxembourg	tel: 352 46 30 35 fax: 352 46 21 85

National technology transfer agencies in some European countries:

France
Agence Nationale de Valorisation   tel: 1 40 17 83 00
de la Recherche (ANVAR),
43 rue de Caumartin,
75436 Paris Cedex 09
France

Germany
Fraunhofer-Gesellschaft,   tel: 0 89 1205-01
Zentralverwaltung,   fax: 0 89 1205-317
Leondrodstrasse 54,
8000 Munchen 19
Germany

Italy
The National Research Council (CNR)   tel: 06/493107-4453337
00185 Roma, P. le Aldo Moro 7,
Italy

Netherlands
Netherlands Organisation for Applied   tel: 31 70 49 65 00
Research (TNO),   fax: 31 70 85 57 00
TNO Corporate Communication Department,
PO Box 297,
2501 BD The Hague,
The Netherlands

References

Abingworth (1989) Abingworth plc Annual Report 1989, London.

Academic/Industrial Collaboration (1977) 'Proceedings of the British/ German seminar on academic research and industry', London: British Council.

Albert, P., Fournier, R. and Marion, S. (1990) 'Developing entrepreneurial attitudes and managment competence among scientists', paper delivered to the European Small Business Seminar, Growing Small Firms – The Role of Technology, Dublin, 11–14 Sept. 1990.

Allen, R. C. (1983) 'Collective invention', *Journal of Economic Behavior and Organization* 4(1): 1–24.

Allesch, J. (1985) 'Innovation centres and science parks in the Federal Republic of Germany: current situation and ingredients for success', in J. M. Gibb (ed.) (1985) *Science Parks and Innovation Centres: their Economic and Social Impact*, Amsterdam: Elsevier.

ANVAR (1989) *Rapport d'Activité 1989*, Paris: ANVAR.

Armstrong, H. E. (1910) *The Teaching of Scientific Method and Other Papers on Education*, 2nd edn, London: Macmillan, p. 257.

Arnold, E. and Guy, K. (1986) *Parallel Convergence: National Strategies in Information Technology*, London: Frances Pinter.

Arthur Young (1988) 'UK Biotech '88', London: Arthur Young.

Axelsson, B. (1987) 'Supplier management and technological development', in H. Hakansson (ed.) (1987) *Industrial Technological Development*, London: Routledge, pp. 128–75.

Baba, M. L. and Hart, S. L. (1986) 'Portrait of a new state initiative in industrial innovation: Michigan's Industrial Technology Institute', in Gray *et al.* (eds) (1986) *Technological Innovation Strategies for a New Partnership*, Amsterdam: Elsevier, pp. 89–112.

Bain, S. (1991) 'Hitech team stalled by bureaucracy', *Scotland on Sunday*, 7 April.

Bain & Co. (1990) 'Innovation in Britain today', London: Bain & Co., October.

Barabaschi, G. (1990) 'Mastering the growth of scientific and technological information', EIRMA Annual Conference Proceedings, Paris: EIRMA.

Beer, J. J. (1959) 'The emergence of the German dye industry', *Illinois*

Studies in the Social Sciences 44, Urbana, Ill.: University of Illinois Press.

Benassi, M. (1991) 'Building blocks for a network process approach', Proceedings of the 7th Industrial Marketing and Purchasing Conference, Uppsala, Sweden, 6-8 September.

Ben-David, J. (1971) *The Scientist's Role in Society - a Comparative Study*, New York: Prentice-Hall.

Bernal, J. D. (1939) *The Social Function of Science*, London: Routledge & Kegan Paul.

Bower, D. J. (1991a) 'Report of a study-visit to Japan, 1989', *Japan Information Service*, London: The Royal Society.

—— (1991b) 'New high technology companies in Europe: 1992 and beyond', *European Research* 2(4): 7-10.

—— (1992) 'Company R&D on campus - US and UK experience', *Long Range Planning*, April.

BP (1989) Annual Report and Accounts, London: BP.

British Biotechnology Group plc (1990) Annual Report and Accounts, Cowley.

BVCA (British Venture Capital Association) (1990) 'Report on investment activity 1989', London: BVCA.

Brock, W. H. (1890) 'The spectrum of scientific patronage' in G. L'E. Turner (ed.) (1976) *Patronage of Science in the Nineteenth Century*, Leiden: Noordhoff International.

BTG (1989) British Technology Group Annual Report 1989, London: BTG.

—— (1990) British Technology Group Annual Report 1990, London: BTG.

Bullock, M. (1983) *Academic Enterprise, Industrial Innovation, and the Development of High Technology Financing in the United States*, London: Brand Brothers & Co.

Burns, T. and Stalker, G. M. (1961) *The Management of Innovation*, London: Tavistock.

Bush, V. (1960) *Science - the Endless Frontier*, Washington DC: NSF.

Business Week (1990) 'Japan - can it catch up in science?', 25 June, pp. 46-59.

Bylinsky, G. (1976) *The Innovative Millionaires*, New York: Charles Scribner.

Cabinet Office (1990) *Annual Review of Government-Funded Research and Development*, London: HMSO.

Cardwell, D. S. L. (1957) *The Organisation of Science in England*, London: Heinemann.

CEST (Centre for Exploitation of Science and Technology) (1991) Annual Review 1990/91, London: CEST.

Childs, W. H. J. and Smart, R. (1966) 'Report on visit to American universities and research institutes', Edinburgh: Heriot-Watt University Archives.

Clark, R. (1985) 'Japan, an independent comment', in M. Bieber (ed.) *Government, Universities and Industry*, London: Economist Publications, pp. 41-3.

Clarke, J. (1989a) 'The economics of the transfer of technology', mimeo, copyright University of Oxford, 28 June.

—— (1989b) 'Research in UK higher education', mimeo, copyright University of Oxford, 11 December.

Cohen, N. (1990) 'Technology', *Financial Times*, 9 August.

Cohen, S. N., Chang, A. C. Y., Boyer, H. W. and Helling, R. B. (1973) 'Construction of biologically functional plasmids in vitro', *Proceedings of the National Academy of Sciences of the USA* 70: 3240.

Coleman, H. D. and Vandenberg, J. D. (1988) *Protecting your Non-US Research in the United States*, New York: DeRosa, Vandenberg & Coleman.

Columbia (1989) 'Statement of policy on proprietary rights in the intellectual products of faculty activity', New York: Trustees of Columbia University, 5 June.

Cornell (1986) 'Proposed statement on objectives for Cornell policy on technology transfer', draft by CRF Long-Range Planning Committee, 23 October.

—— (1989a) 'Cornell Research Foundation Inc.: a Cornell University technology transfer program', Ithaca, NY: CRF Inc.

—— (198b) 'Patent policy', Ithaca NY: Cornell University Board of Trustees, 1 February.

Dang Nguyen, Gaudefroy, J. and Arnold, E. (1985) in M. Sharp (ed.) (1985) *Europe and New Technologies: Six Case Studies in Innovation and Adjustment*, London: Frances Pinter.

Davis, N. (1990) 'Little projects, big ambitions', *Financial Times*, 11 December.

de Jonquières, G. (1990) 'Shortcomings of joint research', *Financial Times*, 16 October.

—— (1991) 'Barriers come tumbling down', *Financial Times*, 11 April.

Dertouzos, M. L. (1989) *Made in America*, Cambridge, Mass.: MIT Press.

DES (Department of Education and Science) (1985) 'The development of higher education into the 1990s', Green Paper, London: HMSO.

Dickson, M. (1991) 'Small is powerful', *Financial Times*, 28 March.

Dorfman, N. (1983) 'Route 128: the development of a regional high technology economy', *Research Policy* 12: 299–316.

DTI (Department of Trade and Industry) (1989) 'Report of the interdepartmental group of the DTI on intellectual property', London: DTI, Sept.

Duby, J.-J. (1985) 'France', in M. Bieber (ed.) (1985) *Government, Universities and Industry*, London: Economist Publications.

Duce, D. A. (ed.) (1984) *Distributed Computing Systems Programme*, London: Peter Peregrinus.

Dupree, A. H. (1957) *Science in the Federal Government*, Cambridge, Mass.: Harvard University Press, pp. 315–23.

EIRMA (1986) 'Developing R&D strategies', Working Group Reports no. 33, Paris: EIRMA.

Englander, A. S., Evenson, R. and Hanazaki, M. (1988) 'R&D, innovation and the total factor productivity slowdown', *OECD Economic Studies* 11, Autumn.

Eveland, J. D. (1985) 'Communication networks in university/industry cooperative research centres', Washington DC: NSF, Division of Industrial Science and Technological Innovation, Productivity Improvement Section.

FHG (1988) Fraunhofer-Gesellschaft Annual Report 1988, English summary, Munich: FHG.

Financial Times, (1990) 'In brief', 11 December.

Fishlock, D. (1990) 'Holding on tight to intellectual property', Financial Times, 26 September.

Fleming, D. (1969) 'Emigré physicists and the biological revolution', in D. Fleming and B. Bailyn (eds) (1969) The Intellectual Migration, Cambridge, Mass.: Harvard University Press.

—— and Bailyn, B. (eds) (1969) The Intellectual Migration, Cambridge, Mass.: Harvard University Press.

Flemings Research (1988) 'Pharmaceutical products worldwide', London: Robert Fleming Securities Ltd.

FoE (The Fellowship of Engineering) (1991) 'The management of technology in United Kingdom manufacturing companies', London: FoE.

Fosdick, R. B. (1952) The Story of the Rockefeller Foundation, New York: Harper.

Fransman, M. (1990) The Market and Beyond: Cooperation and Competition in Information Technology in the Japanese System, Cambridge, England: CUP.

Freeman, C. (1986) 'Introduction' in C. Freeman (ed.) (1986) Design, Innovation and Long Cycles in Economic Development, London: Frances Pinter.

—— (1987) Technology Policy and Economic Performance, London: Frances Pinter.

Freeman, R. (1990) 'Innovation and short-termism', paper delivered at the DTI's conference, London, 25 June.

Gaston, J. (1978) The Reward System in British and American Science, New York: Wiley.

Gaston, R. J. and Bell, S. E. (1990) 'The informal supply of capital', Applied Economics Group, The Office of Economic Research, Small Business Administration, Washington DC.

Geiger, R. L. (1986) To Advance Knowledge, New York/Oxford: Oxford University Press.

Gellman Associates (1976) 'Indications of international trends in technological innovation', report to the National Science Foundation, Washington DC.

Gibb, J. M. (ed.) (1985) Science Parks and Innovation Centres: Their Economic and Social Impact, Amsterdam: Elsevier.

Giersch, G. (1985) 'The growth of science parks', in J. M. Gibb (ed.) (1985) Science Parks and Innovation Centres, Amsterdam: Elsevier, pp. 12–38.

Goerdeler, A. (1985) 'Research cooperation in the Federal Republic of Germany', paper presented to the European Conference on the Cooperation Problem, November.

Grabowski, H. and Vernon, V. (1990) 'The cost of medicine', *Ciba-Geigy Journal*, Basle: Ciba-Geigy.

Gray, D. O., Hetzner, W., Eveland, J. D. and Gidley, T. (1986a) 'NSF's industry/university cooperative research centers program and the innovation process: evaluation-based lessons' in D. O. Gray, T. Solomon and W. Hetzner (eds) (1986) *Technological Innovation – Strategies for a New Partnership*, Amsterdam: Elsevier.

Gray, D. O., Solomon, T. and Hetzner W. (eds) (1986b) *Technological Innovation – Strategies for a New Partnership*, Amsterdam: Elsevier.

Greenlees, A. (1990) 'Tokyo steps up research to beat off "techno-nationalism" ', *The Scotsman*, 27 November.

Griliches, Z. (ed.) (1984) *R&D, Patents and Productivity*, Chicago: Univesity of Chicago Press.

—— Pakes, A. and Hall, B. H. (1986) 'The value of patents as indicators of inventive activity', Harvard Institute of Economic Research, Discussion Paper no. 1285.

Grubb, P. W. (1986) *Patents in Chemistry and Biotechnology*, Oxford: Clarendon Press.

Guy, K., Quintas, P., Hobday, M., Georghiu, L., Cameron, H. and Ray, T. (1991) *Evaluation of the Alvey Programme for Advanced Information Technology*, London: HMSO.

Haeussler, H. W. (1987) 'Universities, industry and intellectual property rights', paper given at Regional Seminar on Licensing and other Technology Transfer Arrangements, World Intellectual Property Organization in co-operation with the Office of Patents Administration, Seoul, October.

Håkansson, H. (1982) *International Marketing and Purchasing of Industrial Goods: an Interactive Approach*, Chichester: John Wiley.

—— (1987) 'Product development in networks', in H. Håkansson (ed.) *Industrial Technological Development*, London: Routledge, pp. 84–124.

—— (1989) *Corporate Technological Behaviour*, London: Routledge.

Hancock, E. (1983) 'Academe meets industry: charting the bottom line', *Alumni Magazine Consortium* 7: 1–9.

Hare, P., Lauchlan, J. and Thompson, M. (1989) *An Assessment of ESPRIT in the UK*, Edinburgh: Technological Change Research Centre, Heriot-Watt University.

Harvard (1986) 'Statement of policy in regard to inventions, patents and copyrights', President and Fellows of Harvard College, Cambridge, Mass., March.

—— (1987) 'Guide to patents', President and Fellows of Harvard College, Cambridge, Mass.

—— (1988) 'Principal investigator's handbook', Harvard University Office for Sponsored Research, Cambridge, Mass., September.

Harvey, I. (1990) 'Holding on tight to intellectual property', *Financial Times*, 26 September.

Heaton, H. (1948) *Economic History of Europe*, New York: Harper Brothers.

Hector, G. (1985) 'A tough slog for venture capitalists', *Fortune* 8(2): 74.

Henderson, P. (1977) 'Two British errors: their probable size and some possible lessons', *Oxford Economic Papers* 29: 159–215.

HMSO (1989) *Annual Review of Government-Funded R&D 1989*, London: HMSO.

Hofstadter, R. and Smith, W. (1961) *American Higher Education: a Documentary History*, vol. 2, Chicago: Chicago University Press, pp. 568–9.

IAB (Innovation Advisory Board) (1990) *Innovation: City Attitudes and Practice*, London: Department of Trade and Industry.

INSERM (1991) 'L'INSERM et la création des entreprises', Paris: INSERM: 22 January.

Irvine, J. (1988) *Evaluating Applied Research: Lessons from Japan*, London/New York: Pinter.

Jack, A. (1990) 'Suitable cases for treatment', *Financial Times*, 14 October.

James, R. (1990) 'Equity funding gap', *Nostrum* 10, April, p. 7.

Japan Economic Journal (1984) *High-Tech Start-up Ventures in Japan*, Tokyo: Nihon Keizai Shimbun Inc.

Jenkins, L. (1988) 'Routes to exploitation', paper delivered to the Royal Society of Medicine, 16 March.

Kendrick, J. W. and Vaccara, B. N. (1980) *New Developments in Productivity Measurement and Analysis*, Chicago: University of Chicago Press.

Killian, J. R. (1985) *The Education of a College President*, Cambridge, Mass.: MIT Press.

Kodama, F., Nishioka, S., Osada, H. and Kurita, M. (1981) 'Possibilities for establishing a research evaluation system in Japan', report to Science and Technology Agency, Tokyo: Asahi Research Centre.

Köhler, G. and Milstein, C. (1975) 'Continuous cultures of fused cells secreting antibody of predefined specificity', *Nature* 256: 495.

KTEC (Kansas Technology Enterprise Corporation) (1989) KTEC Annual Report 1989, Kansas: Topeka.

Laage-Hellman, J. (1987) 'Process innovation through technical cooperation', in H. Håkansson (ed.) Industrial Technological Development, London: Routledge, pp. 26–77.

Laffitte, P. (1985) 'Sophia Antipolis: a science city', in J. M. Gibb (ed.) (1985) *Science Parks and Innovation Centres*, Amsterdam: Elsevier, pp. 25–31.

Larsen, J. K. (1984) 'Policy alternatives and the semiconductor industry', report to the NSF, Los Altos, Ca.: Cognos Associates.

Lederman, L. M. (1969) 'A great collaboration', *Science* 164: 169.

Lester, R. M. (1941) *Forty Years of Carnegie Giving*, New York: Scribners.

McCauley, M. and Zimmer, S. (1989) 'Explaining international differences in the cost of capital', *Federal Reserve Bank of New York Quarterly Review*, Summer, pp. 7–28.

MacKenzie, I. and Jones, R. R. (1985) *Universities and Industry*, special Report no. 213, London: Economist Intelligence Unit, Economist Publications.

Mansfield, E. (1986) 'Patents and innovation: an empirical study', *Management Science*, February.

—— (1991) 'Academic research and industrial innovation', *Research Policy* 20: 1–12.

Merton, R. K. (1973) *The Sociology of Science: Theoretical and Empirical Investigations*, ed. N. W. Storer, Chicago: University of Chicago Press.

Meyerhoff (1982) 'Campus research', *San Francisco Examiner*, 26 March.

MIT (1988) *Guide to the Ownership, Distribution and Commercial Development of MIT Technology*, Cambridge, Mass.: MIT Press.

Moffat, S. (1991) 'Picking Japan's research brains', *Fortune*, 25 March, pp. 84–96.

MORI (1989) 'The business of invention', a survey carried out for the BTG by MORI, London: British Technology Group.

Moritani, M. (1991) *Japanese Technology*, Tokyo: Simul Press.

Moses, V. (1985) 'Industrial confidentiality and academic freedom: accommodation or contradiction?', in M. Bieber (ed.) (1985) *Government, Universities and Industry*, London: Economist Publications.

Murray, G. (1990) 'Change and maturity in the British venture capital industry', London: British Venture Capital Association.

NAO (National Audit Office) (1988) *Department of Trade and Industry: the Alvey Programme for Advanced Information Technology*, London: HMSO.

Nature (1990a) 'News and views', 348: 7.

—— (1990b) 'Radical computing in Japan', 347: 217.

—— (1990c) 'What electronic future for Europe?', 367: 695.

NEDO (National Economic Development Office) (1990) *The Innovation Management Tool Kit*, London: HMSO.

Nelsen, L. L. (1988a) *Research Collaboration between Industry and the University: Making it Work*, Cambridge, Mass.: MIT Press.

—— (1988b) 'Intellectual property and the university', mimeo, copyright Massachusetts Institute of Technology.

NIBB (1988) Annual Report of the National Institute of Basic Biology, Okazaki, Japan.

Northern Echo (1990) Special advertising supplement: 'Belasis Hall Technology Park, a joint initiative by ICI and English Estates North', September.

NSF (National Science Foundation) (1986) 'Technology in retrospect and critical events in science', Illinois Institute of Technological Research, National Science Foundation, NSF-C535, Washington DC, December.

Oakley, B. and Owen, K. (1989) *Alvey: Britain's Strategic Computing Initiative*, Cambridge, Mass.: MIT Press.

OECD (1990) *Main Science and Technology Indicators*, Paris: OECD.

Paine Webber Inc. (1989) *The Biotechnology Tape Reader* vol. II, no. 11, New York, November.

Pajaro (1982) Pajaro Dunes Biotechnology Conference Statement, *Tech Talk*, 7 April.

Pavitt, K. (ed.) (1980) *Technical Innovation and British Economic Performance*, London: Macmillan.

—— and Soete, L. (1980) 'Innovative activities and export shares', in K. Pavitt (ed.) (1980) *Technical Innovation and British Economic Performance*, London: Macmillan, pp. 38–66.

Peters, D. H. and Roberts, E. B. (1969) 'Unutilised items in university laboratories', *Academy of Management Journal*, June.

Phillips, G. O. (1989) *Innovation and Technology Transfer in Japan and Europe*, London/New York: Routledge.

Pisano, G. P. (1991) 'The governance of innovation: vertical integration and collaborative arrangements in the biotechnology industry', *Research Policy* 19: 237-49.

Plender, J. (1990) 'Malaise in need of a longterm remedy', *Financial Times*, 20 July.

PREST/SPRU (1987) 'Evaluation of the Alvey Programme: interim report', London: HMSO, October.

Raub, W. (1981) Testimony before Committee on Science and Technology, US House of Representatives, 8-9 June 1981, on Commercialisation of Academic Biomedical Research, Washington DC: US Govt Printing Office, 77-87.

Redwood, A., Stella, M. E., Lewin, T. E., Depenbusch, D. and Maygers, D. (1989) 'Technology transfer and industrial liaison for Kansas economic development' Report no. 161, Institute for Public Policy and Business Research, University of Kansas.

Redwood, A. L. (1991) 'Technology transfer and university-industry liaison to underpin private sector innovation and competitiveness in West Germany and the United Kingdom', Report no. 184, Institute for Public Policy and Business Research, University of Kansas.

Reimers, N. (1980) 'Survey of directed mechanisms for innovation of university research', *Les Nouvelles* 55(2).

—— (1987) 'Tiger by the tail', *CHEMTECH*, August, pp. 464-71.

—— (1988) 'Commercialization of ideas in a research environment', Stanford, Ca., Office of Technology Licensing, 13 October.

Roberts, E. B. (1968) 'A basic study of innovations', *Research Management*, July.

Rockefeller (1985) 'Policy of the Rockefeller University on industrial sponsorship of research', New York: Office of the President, Rockefeller University, May.

—— (1986) 'The Rockefeller University policy on external service, consulting and conflicts of interest involving members of the faculty', New York: Rockefeller University, 18 April.

Roericht, R. (1985) 'University industry relations in West Germany: problems and prospects', in M. Bieber (ed.) (1985) *Government, Universities and Industry*, London: Economist Publications.

Rogers, E. M. (1982) 'Information exchange and technological innovation', in D. Sahal (ed.) *The Transfer and Utilization of Technical Knowledge*, Lexington, Mass.: Lexington Books.

—— (1986) 'The role of the research university in the spinoff of high technology companies', *Technovation* 4: 169-81.

Rosenzweig, R. M. (1982) *The Research Universities and their Patrons*, Berkeley: University of California Press.

Salomon, J.-J. (1973) *Science and Politics*, London: Macmillan.

Saxenian, A. (1983) 'The genesis of Silicon Valley', *Built Environment* 9(1): 7-17.

Schankerman, M. and Pakes, A. (1985) 'Estimates of the value of patent rights in European countries during the post-1950s period', *Economic Journal*, December.

Scheidegger, A. (1990) 'Catching the tide of innovation', *Nature* 348: 576.

Scherer, F. M. (1983) 'The propensity to patent', *International Journal of Industrial Organisation* 11: 227-45.

—— (1984) 'Using linked patent and R&D data to measure interindustry technology flows', in Z. Griliches (ed.) (1984) *R&D, Patents and Productivity*, Chicago: University of Chicago Press.

Schmid, R. D. (1991) 'Biotechnology-related "Research Associations" in Japan', *Biotech Forum Europe*, April, vol. 8: 166-70.

Schrader, S. (1991) 'Informal technology transfer between firms: co-operation through informal trading', *Research Policy* 20: 153-70.

Science (1982) 'The academic/industry complex', *Science* 216: 960-1.

SCST (1991), House of Lords Select Committee for Science and Technology, 'Innovation in Manufacturing Industry', vol. I, report of 29 Jan., London: HMSO.

Segal, N. S. (1987) 'Emergence and growth of the Cambridge phenomenon', paper presented at a conference on Technopolis: Emerging Issues in Technology Commercialisation and Economic Development, Austin, Texas, February.

Segal Quince Wicksteed (1988) *Universities, Enterprise and Local Economic Development*, Manpower Services Commission, London: HMSO.

Senker, J. and Sharp, M. (1988) 'The Biotechnology Directorate of the SERC: report and evaluation of its achievements, 1981-1987', Science Policy Research Unit, University of Sussex, Brighton, March.

Servos, J. W. (1980) 'The industrial relations of science: Chemical Engineering at MIT, 1900-39', *ISIS* 71: 531-49.

Sharp, M. (1989) 'European technology: does 1992 matter?', no. 19, Papers in Science, Technology and Public Policy, Science Policy Research Unit, University of Sussex, Brighton.

Shennan, F. (1990) 'Venture capital plan to plug the funding gap', *The Sunday Times*, Scotland, 21 October.

Spriano, G. (1989) 'R&D networks: the emerging market for technological and scientific services', in A. Bressand and K. Nicolaidis (eds) (1989) *Strategic Trends in Services*, New York: Harper & Row.

Sproull, R. L. (1985) 'The USA', in M. Bieber (ed.) (1985) *Government, Universities and Industry*, London: Economist Publications.

Stankiewicz, R. (1986) *Academics and Entrepreneurs*, London: Frances Pinter.

Stoffaes, C. (1984) 'French industrial strategy in sunrise sectors', in Z. Griliches (ed.) (1984) *R&D, Patents and Productivity*, Chicago: University of Chicago Press.

Storz, K. A. (1985) 'Technology promotion, a challenge for credit institutions, illustrated by way of Technologiezentrum Stuttgart', in J. M. Gibb (ed.) (1985) *Science Parks and Innovation Centres*, Amsterdam: Elsevier.

Swinbanks, D. (1990) 'The taxman's human face', *Nature* 347: 703.

THES (1991) 'UFC to revise research ranks', *Times Higher Education Supplement*, 5 July.

Tornatzky, L. D., Eveland, J. D., Hetzner, W. A., Johnson, A., Roitman, D. and Schneider, J. (1983) 'The process of technological innovation: reviewing the literature', Washington DC: NSF.

Turner, F. M. (1980) 'Public science in Britain', *ISIS* 71: 589–608.

Turner, G. L'E. (ed.) (1976) *Patronage of Science in the Nineteenth Century*, Leiden: Noordhoff International.

Twiss, B. and Goodridge, M. (1989) *Managing Technology for Competitive Advantage*, London: Pitman.

von Hippel, E. (1988) *The Sources of Innovation*, New York: Oxford University Press.

Wade, N. (1977) 'Recombinant DNA:NIH rules broken in insulin gene project', *Science* 197: 1342–6.

Wallard, A. (1984) 'The problematic relationship between research and policy', in M. Gibbons, P. Gummett and B. M. Udgaonkar (eds) *Science and Technology Policy for the 1980s and Beyond*, London: Longman.

Waugaman, P. G. (1986) 'Encouraging innovation in North Carolina', in Gray *et al.* (eds) (1986) *Technological Innovation Strategies for a New Partnership*, Amsterdam: Elsevier.

Weisbach, J. A. and Burke, H. T. (1990) 'Patents and technology transfer', *TIBTECH* 8: 31–5.

Whittaker, E. and Bower, D. J. (1991) 'Heriot-Watt Business School working paper no. 3', Edinburgh: Heriot-Watt University.

Yamauchi, I. (1986) 'Longrange R&D' in C. Freeman (ed.) (1986) *Design, Innovation and Long Cycles in Economic Development*, London: Pinter.

Index

www.ingramcontent.com/pod-product-compliance
Ingram Content Group UK Ltd.
Pitfield, Milton Keynes, MK11 3LW, UK
UKHW020858280225
455677UK00006B/89